SECRET ENEMIES

OF

TRUE REPUBLICANISM,

MOST IMPORTANT DEVELOPMMENTS REGARDING THE INNER LIFE OF MAN AND THE SPIRIT WORLD, IN ORDER TO ABOLISH REVOLUTIONS AND WARS AND TO ESTABLISH PERMANENT PEACE ON EARTH,

ALSO:

THE PLAN FOR REDEMPTION OF NATIONS FROM MONARCHICAL AND OTHER OPPRESIVE SPECULATIONS AND FOR THE INTRODUCTION OF THE PROMISED NEW ERA OF HARMONY, TRUTH AND RIGHTEOUSNESS ON THE WOHLE GLOBE.

WRITTEN BY

ANDREW B. SMOLNIKAR,

FORMERLY EIGHTEEN YEARS PRIEST BENEDICTINE MONK AND IMPERIAL ROYAL PROFESSOR OF BIBICAL LITERATURE; AFTERWARDS SINCE A. D. 1838, BY SIGNS ACCORDING TO PROPHECIES DECLARED AND CONFIRMED REPRESENTATIVE OF MESSENGERS FOR THE INTRODUCTION OF THE UNIVERSAL REPUBLIC, COMMONLY ALTHOUGH IMPROPERLY CALLED THE MILLENNIUM.

PUBLISHED BY ROBERT D. ELDRIDGE,
Springhill, Peace Union Centre.
POST OFFICE DONNALLY'S MILL, PERRY CO.: PA.
1859.

PRELIMINARY REMARKS.

Attentive readers will find superabundance of signs or credentials testifying the mission of every one who comprehends this book and acts with us for the accomplishment of the great promise, if they peruse the whole book as often as necessary for a full understanding of each event mentioned herein in connexion with the whole. From this connection of events it is evident, that in collisions in to which we have come with our opposers during the performance of the duties of our mission, we were under the direction of those invisible guardians who are labouring to introduce the promised new era of Truth and Righteousness, while our opposers were endeavouring to support the existing systems of delusion and iniquity, and that spirits of all spheres, heavenly angels as well as infernal demons, give testimony to our mission, spirits of each sphere in such a manner as is most suitable to their sphere. By the developments made in this book the secret enemies of true Republicanism are made manifest, and it is made clear, how every party and sect, notwithstanding their profession of republicanism, are supporting Popery, or, what is the same Monarchy, if they disregard our disclosures concerning the Roman Catholic and the Protestant churches in reference to Christ's Peaceable Reign which will be the universal republic of truth and rightousness, and if they neglect to co-operate with us for its introduction.

When I say "us," I understand the whole body of messengers whom I represent. I became Representative of this Body by having performed and explained what has been shown to me by the Spirit of Truth for the introduction of the promised New Era. No imaginations, but facts, events, are testifying our Heavenly Mission for the true Freedom, Harmony and Peace of Nations, as well as the infernal Mission of those who either openly or secretly, are opposed to our mission. In this their condition they are supporting the Papal Imperial Royal or Monarchial powers. This will be evident to those who comprehend this book. Then they will know that those are either wittingly deceivers, or are deceived and repeat the lies and slanders of others, who say that I make too great claims and am anxious to be a great man. I confess to be nothing else but a true republican, a man for free discussion, testifying what I know, and offering it to be duly examined and used for the welfare of nations. I had to forsake all things of this world and to devote all my time to deep investigations, till at length my studies had arrived to maturity, that I could be used by Heavenly Powers as an instrument or medium to disclose what is required for Christ's peaceable Reign on Earth. But those who should have been our first labourers in the great cause of Human Redemption, have deceived others in regard to our mission; and I have been abused, slandered and persecuted, and have suffered more than a man could willingly bear for his fellow men, without being supported by Higher Powers. This support has brought me on the ground where I stand, and on which they shall arrive who will study this book with uderstanding, and then act accordingly.

This book is divided into several treatises, which are so connected that every reader in order to comprehend the unexpected developments for the introduction of the promised New Era, must study them in the order in which they appear. While studying in this manner, if the contents of some passage appear to him not only unexpected, but also very improbable, he will receive more light upon them in the continuation of studying this book, till at length that which appeared at the first view improbable, will be made manifest to him to be a great truth, and he will become our zealous fellow labourer in the great mission for the accomplishment of the greatest Promises to the Human race. I write in the expectation, that my brethren and sisters, after having perused this book, will comprehend their calling and act accordingly with their sincere servant,

ANDREW B. SMOLNIKAR.

Washington D. C. March 29th, 1859.

Remark:

I wrote this preface in the expectation of soon finding in Washington means for publishing this book. But I had to wait, till at length the war in Italy commenced. Therefore readers are requested to study what they must know to stop Revolutions and Wars and to commence the New Era of Harmony and Peace.

FIRST TREATISE.

Louis Napoleon, according to a severe divine judgment Emperor of France, and James Buchanan, according to the merciful divine benignity President of the United States.

On the 27th January, 1859, while I was ready to start from Philadelphia, a messenger said, that on that day an article appeared in the German Democrat of that city for my use, and handed to me the number containing that article, from which we translate the following passages:

"A pamphlet of the famous Mr. Belly, directed to Emperor Napoleon III, was announced in Paris on all corners of the streets with very large letters, under the inscription

NAPOLEON AND BUCHANAN.

"Whereas nothing can be published in Paris without the permission of the Imperial censorship, it is supposed, that Mr. Belly acted according to a superior order to arouse the public opinion against the United States. The President's message gives the pretext for it. The United States are represented as deadly enemies of the whole Latin Race and of the monarchies of Europe, which must fall to their feet, if that race does not commence a crusade against the heretics, and take the sword against the pirates, thieves and bankrupts of the United States."

Not having the original of the pamphlet and giving the following passages in a free translation from the German translation which appeared in the above quoted number of the Democrat, I may be excused by those who have the French pamphlet at hand, if they should find any deviation from it. Monsieur Belly writes besides other things also:

"The longing of the United States for Cuba and Mexico has not only the tendency to enlarge their territory and their interests, but they act besides this, according to a principle, which is diametrically opposite to that of France; they do not care about any civilization beyond their frontier; they have made alliance with all who are filled with hatred against the European politics. When the Democratic Republic obtains the supremacy in the new world, all empires and kingdoms in the world will become inimical to its interests and therefore it will be consequent and necessary to destroy them either by art or by force..... Our commerce, our industry will be compelled to obey instead of being the rulers, and the discovery of the new world will lead to the remarkable result of having occasioned the death of the old.

"The Catholic sovereigns constituted by God and by their subjects, are obliged to introduce such circumstances as to carry into execution their legitimate claims. And those who have been elected by a band without discipline, by bankrupts and thieves, dare to declare publicly, that the hour has come for these thieves and bankrupts to attack the civilized world! are we not as much devoted to the truth, as they are to the lie? We should not delay to promote our system of salvation, while we are discussing their system of perdition. And whereas they are elevating the crime to their religion with more energy than we do our holy religion, while we appear to surrender it, we will henceforth extol the cross and draw the sword, and unite the Latin race to the alliance, without which there is no salvation for civilization.

"The president's message is in open opposition to the faith, the ideas, the principles and the interests, the acknowledged defender of which your Majesty is. That message strikes Europe on both cheeks; and I affirm that those who like to make it laughable, become pale when they reflect upon it in their closets

"Mr. Buchanan and the nation whom he represents, keep these things not any longer in secret. From henceforth they demand Cuba, and the language in the message shows, that they will not desist from any means to obtain their object. This object is one portion of Mexico and then an other, the whole Central America and West Indies," &c.

If our profession which is expressed on the title page of this book, is true, we have received the commission to move nations and their rulers to establish the universal republic of truth and justice, harmony and peace. It will be the true reign of Christ, for which all political and ecclesiastical memorable events of past centuries and of this time, are preparations. Our commission, that is, the commission of messengers whom I represent, is confirmed by so many signs according to prophecies, that while I was writing the last of the five German volumes which have been published from A. D. 1838 till 1842, I have oftentimes repeated, that the key has been given in those volumes to unlock and explain so many prophecies and signs testifying our mission, that five hundred volumes could be filled, if there had not been superabundance of them already published in the five above mentioned volumes, from which it is evident, that neither monarchs amongst themselves in Europe, nor political and ecclesiastical parties and sects in this country, can establish peace, but will continue to quarrel and consume every year an enormous amount of property for war preparations, and corrupt and ruin nations, and destroy many men and women during those preparations, till at length they are again and again so brutalized and enraged, that they kill each other, till all parties are so exhausted, that they are compelled to make peace, which is nothing else but an armistice; because when the true peace or Christ's reign, which will be the universal Republic of Truth and Justice, shall be established on the whole globe, soldiers and all preparations for war, will disappear, and those who are now learning how to destroy each other, will learn how to prolong their lives and improve their intellectual and moral faculties for their own temporal and eternal welfare, as well as for the welfare of others. Wo! wo! wo! to the Roman catholics as well as others in these United States and in all other parts of America and in Europe and elsewhere, if the infernal fire of revolution and war, which is glowing, breaks out with all force in the United States of America. It would extend on the globe and consume millions of men, and amongst them also Monarchs. But we write to prevent their destruction, and to prepare them to become true republicans and truly happy, and to contribute their share for the happiness of all men.

After the publication of the above mentioned five volumes I made urgent applications to political and ecclesiastical rulers and their counsellors in Europe by sending to some of them my books and letters, and to others letters only, showing how to obtain my books, and exhorting them to study them and act accordingly to prevent revolutions and wars and to commence the new Era. After that, whenever a peculiar crisis was approaching, we have issued some publication, warning the American Nation as well as other nations and their governments, and showing, that there was high time to study the contents of *our* volumes. I am not alone, but there are invisible messengers giving testimony by my instrumentality, as superabundance of proof is given also in this volume. In this connection of matters I mention the following instance:

At the end of the year 1853 my pamphlet "Antichristian Conspiracy against true Republicanism" issued from the press; and in the first part of the year 1854 copies of that pamphlet as well as written disclosures containing most solemn warnings to the American as well as to all other nations, were sent to President Pierce and to a number of congressmen in both houses. In said pamphlet and in the annexed written disclosures, the Government was most solemnly exhorted to appoint a convention for examining our system or the magnetic chain of events through the course of the past centuries in connection with the events of this generation, which have not been understood so as they are made manifest in our chain for binding the Dragon, the spirit of delusion and destruction, Revel. xx. 2. who has given his power, aud his seat, and great authority Revel. xiii: 2, not only to the representative of the beast or the Pope of Rome, but also to the ten horns of the beast, or kings, that is monarchs, who hate the whore, that is the Apostatized Church, the people who have apostatized from truth and justice, and whom monarchs make desolate and naked, and eat their flesh and burn them with fire, Revel. xvii: 16.

"The Catholic Sovereigns" are according to the quoted passage of Mr. Belly, "constituted by God and by their subjects" The number of the Democrat, which occasioned this treatise, was providentially handed to me. But here is no room to explain that which will be explained in our "monthly theological course," which is appointed in this book, and in which our system or the chain to bind the dragon, will be exhibited, and in which will be made manifest, how far "the Catholic sovereigns" or monarchs are constituted by their subjects, and how their subjects would constitute them, if they were free and enlightened, as they should be according to the will of God who has endowed them with intellectual and moral faculties, to be duly developed. Here we mention only, that the highest duty of monarchs is to do all in their power for that development. If monarchs would fulfil their highest duty, their subjects would become true republicans, and then monarchs would cease to be, what they now are by the appointment of the dragon, the spirit of delusion and destruction, by whose inspiration they are executioners of the degraded people whose education has been neglected, and who would have become true republicans, if monarchs had become fathers and teachers of the ignorant. But obviously appears to be as absurd, as Mr. Belly's assertion, that God has constituted the monarchs, although it is manifest, that the dragon has constituted them, or they are constituted "according to a severe divine judgment," according to his eternal laws, when people are so degraded, that they are not prepared for a better government, what is expressed in the following words of the Revelation ; "God has put in the hearts of the ten horns to fulfil his will, and agree, and give their kingdom unto the beast, until the words of God shall be fulfilled," REVEL. XVII.: 17.

In those circumstances, after the destruction, of the first Napoleon's power, it was best, when the rulers or fathers of nations have neglected to fulfil their highest duty, that they have submitted their monarchies under the protection of the Pope, the representative of the Beast with ten horns and seven heads, till the prophecy has been fulfilled. From neglecting that rule much greater evils, most dreadful revolutions and wars originated. The history of the so called christian church, when some portions rebelled against the Pope through the course of centuries until this time, is the most horrible theatre under the dominion of the dragon. Therefore, after the destruction of the first Napoleon we read in REVEL. xvii :

13, that the ten horns or monarchs agreed unanimously (in the Congress of Vienna, A. D. 1815,) to give their power and strength unto the beast, that is, to make the Pope, the representative of the beast, a partaker of their own power and strength. This was the means for the support of their own thrones, till the prophecy has been fulfilled by what has been executed through our mediumships in the Roman Catholic Church, and has been explained in the first three of my above mentioned five German volumes. Those three volumes appeared between A. D. 1838 and 1840, and have been sent to three Roman Catholic Monarchs, to wit, the Emperor of Austria, the King of Bavaria and the King of France, with my hand writings, showing to the first two their highest duty to enjoin their Theologians to examine those volumes and to send to me the result of their examinations, to be published with my remarks, that truth might be made manifest, and to the king of France, that he should translate those volumes into French and spread them as much as possible in his monarchy. All three have been most solemnly exhorted to do what was required in those volumes to prevent the repetition of revolutions, wars and other plagues, which cannot be removed but must be repeated, till the heavenly message of Peace made manifest by our instrumentality, is received by governments and nations. When our applications to and exhortations of political and ecclesiastical influential men in America and in Europe were not regarded, and in these days of Noah the earth was corrupt and filled with violence, and all flesh had corrupted his way, I Mos. vi: 11 and 12, the flood of revolution broke out in Europe in the year 1848, on the exact day in correspondence with prophecies given by our instrumentality and published in my volumes, and emperors and kings, and their machines of destruction, the bishops of America and in Europe, and other political and ecclesiastical officers, who with all our exhortations remained obstinate sinners against the Holy Ghost, who has disclosed by our instrumentality that which is required for the introduction of the promised peaceable reign of Christ, which according to our disclosures by a long chain of signs according to prophecies, will be the universal republic of truth and justice, harmony and peace on the whole globe, are responsible for all destruction of human life and property, which were consumed in that revolution and afterwards until this hour, and would have been saved, if the means shown in our message, had been used.

Ferdinand, Emperor of Austria, was the first compelled to give a constitution. I read it on the 18th, April, 1848, and was inspired to write on the 19th, April, or, on his birth-day a letter to him and an appeal to the inhabitants of the Austrian Empire, assuring them, that the calamities came, because the contents of our publications had not been regarded, although our mission had been superabundantly proven by signs according to prophecies. I confessed also, that I was ready to go instantly to Vienna, and to show practically, how to make the right use of that constitution for the commencement of the new era of harmony and peace, if the emperor would publish directly my appeal to the inhabitants of his empire, and write to me, and give the security to support the constitution, which was such as the inhabitants of the empire had a right to demand, as well as the emperor had a right to watch against the abuse and to apply the proper means for the right use of the constitution.

My former applications and my volumes have been sent by me directly through Triest to Vienna, but that my last document to emperor Ferdinand was sent to his minister in Washington city with an urgent exhortation to the minister, to forward it to the emperor, and with the remark that in the time in which an answer could be expected, I would send to the minister my direction, to which post office he had to send the answer; because I wrote to the emperor from the State of New-York on my journey to other States. I wrote at length to the minister, that if he receives an answer to my documents from the Emperor Ferdinand, he should send it to the post office of Nashville, capital of the State of Tennessee. I urged the Emperor to send an answer as soon as possible, and I assured him, that it was impossible, to prevent new revolutions without the use of the remedy contained in our message of peace. But knowing the slowness of the business at the Austrian government, I new on the 14th September 1848, at noon time to the post office of Nashville to ask for letters. When I was approaching the post office, fire bells commenced to arouse people who were asking where the fire was. Some answered, that it was in the Presbyterian Church on Church street; but others remarked, that they should not be mocked in this manner; because it appeared to be quite improbable, that fire should break out at that hour in that season in a church without being struck by lightning; and that was a very clear day.

I asked in the post office for letters. But there was no letter for me there. On my return from the post office, the whole presbyterian church the largest in that city, on Church Street, was enveloped in awful flames, by which it was entirely consumed.

The next night after that solemn spectacle an angel of my Lord brought to me the message, (and attentive readers of this book will be convinced, that when my mission requires, I come in perceivable communication with Heavenly messengers,) that on the next sunday I should proclaim in that city, that that was a prophetical fire testifying that revolutions would break out again in the Austrian empire, because the bishops of that empire had neglected to fulfil their highest duty to instruct the Emperor in what he should do for the pacification of nations, and that the revolution should be a solemn warning to the citizens of the United States: because judgments cannot be removed from this country, but must increase till churches of the great harlot and her daughters will be consumed, if these judgments shall not be stopped by the application of our message of peace. Public halls are generally not opened for our proclamations, because we have no money to pay for their use. But at that time the masonic fraternity were carrying their instruments into their building, from which they removed them during the danger while the church opposite their building was burning. I said to them, that I had to proclaim a message against the Pope of Rome in correspondence with that fire, and requested them to grant their hall for that purpose, They granted it, and my proclamation was advertised in the daily newspapers of Nashville. It was delivered on the next sunday after the fire in the German language before, and in the English language after noon.

In the next month after that proclamation the last dreadful European revolution and war commenced in Hungary in correspondence with the fact, that the bishops of Hungary were the last among the bishops of Europe, who have been under the direction of my Heavenly leaders most solemnly warned to prevent the revolution which commenced in Paris on the 24th Febuary, 1848. That was in the octave of the tenth anniversary after my first public appearance in my present mission and my solemn initiation by Heavenly messengers for this mission. Ten years in commemoration of the ten horns of the beast were granted for repentance to the blind leaders of the blind, for whom I published A. D 1838 the first volume of explanations of the mystery; and in that year I commenced to exhort Emperor Ferdinand and his bishops, that they should study that volume. But after the publication of the fifth volume A.D. 1842, the bishops of Hungary were the last amongst the grandees of Europe, to whom I applied; to wit, when all my applications were disregarded, I published a Latin circular and sent copies of it to a number of bishops in Europe. While I was preparing those copies for the mail, Samuel Ludvigh, a Hungarian scholar, came into my room. He never before nor after that did come to me, although I met with him several times in other places, and warned him always, that he should study my writings to be converted from his materialism to the true spiritualism. But at that my meeting with him in my room I said to him, that he came at the right time, to give me directions to all bishops in Hungary. He did so, and by this unexpected provision I was enabled, to send to all Roman Catholic bishops in Hungary copies of my Latin circular, in which direction to find copies of my volumes, was given and the duty of the Austrian bishops was shown to study my volumes, and then to instruct the Emperor and other grandees of the Austrian Empire and Hungarian Kingdom, in what they should do, to prevent revolutions and wars, and to establish the promised peace on earth.

When all our endeavoring to move the blind leaders of the blind to take the medicine which was prepared in our pnblications to open their eyes, was disregarded, I met at length in Cincinnati with the same doctor Samuel Ludvigh, a materialistic reformer, trusting in weapons of war, and I was inspired that I said to him, that there was high time for him to learn that he had an immortal soul and also, that he himself was a strong medium of deluding and destroying spirits, and that I was ready to give him a peculiar testimony of that truth most necessary for him to become an apostle of peace. He asked, how I could show him this. He was not ready to examine arguments and experience of others in this respect. Therefore I, according to the direction of my Heavenly leader, said, that I would magnetize him. That was the same in that connection of things, as to say, that I would initiate him into the mystery of our close connection with departed spirits. There is the right use as well as the abuse of human magnetism. Some eight years ago I published a pamphlet on "the dreadful abuse of human magnetism in the mysteries of the Roman Catholic Church and her daughters the protestant sects." Samuel Ludvigh was willing that I should magnetize him directly. But I remarked, that the tavern in which I met with him, was not the proper place for our initiation or ordination. But he was inspired to ask me, that I should make a trial there in his room in which some of his materialists were with him. I was impressed to do so, and it was directly made manifest, that the legion of demons by which he was surrounded, were compelled to give way to our magnetism. And when he fell into the magnetic sleep, I said to him, that to go so deep into our magnetism as to be convinced of man's immortality and to become with us an apostle of the New Era, he must visit me at my boarding house. And he promised to do so on the next following evening. I said that I would come to take him with me. But when I came I found not him, but a writing in which he imformed me, that some friends came and moved him to start with them for other places. We heard then, that he had started for Europe. At length we received his German pamphlet, which was published in Hamburgh, a seaport in Europe, and was entitled: "The sword of Revolution," in which this strange prophet Samuel Ludvigh, reports, that he took a sword of the American revolution and other insignia of war, and copies of his German periodical, entitled "The Torch," and stopped in Europe first in Paris, and three days after his departure from that city, revolution broke out there. From thence he went to Berlin, and from that city to Vienna, and in each of those cities soon after his departure revolution broke out. At length he put his sword and other insignia of war into the National Museum of Hungary, and returned to America.

Those who will study this whole book so as to comprehend the whole connection of matters, will learn gradually better than they see when they arrive in reading it to this period, that my meeting with Samuel Ludvigh in Cincinnati was providentially prepared for a testimony to all governments, that when Samuel Ludvigh who had performed since A. D. 1838 in his meetings with me manifold prophetical actions which have been mentioned in some of my former publications, and was also at that my meeting with him in Cincinnati not yet disposed to become an apostle of peace, and the measure of crimes in Europe was filled, the Heavenly congress with whom we are connected, gave permission to the infernal demons to carry their medium with the war insignia to Europe, and to announce to the infernal demons in Europe, that the time had arrived for them to inspire their mediums to break out in their fury and spread destruction, for the reason that those who kept people in bondage and were the cause of their degredation, have rejected our message of peace and continued to be obstinate sinners against the Holy Ghost who has offered them in our publications the means for the pacification of nations. But whereas the means for peace were not used, revolutions and wars had to give a new turn to human affairs.

When those who were deluding the good natured Emperor Ferdinand, kept him in bondage and would not make use of my above mentioned last application to him for a commencement of the millennial happiness first in the Austrian Empire, I, according to the direction of my Heavenly Leaders, made no more applications to Europe, but commenced to urge Presidents and other influential men at the government of the United States, to study our message and the credentials of our mission for the pacification of nations. When after all my applications to several of the predecessors of President Pierce at length also he remained in the shackles of the infernal Papal Imperial Royal Magnetism, and members of the Congress of all parties and sects followed his example, I was impressed that I should apply to the Emperor Louis Napoleon and to prepare him, that he might commence to look, where to find the great refuge for his own and the true happiness of his family in their mortal bodies as well as in all eternity after their departure from this short life, every moment of which should be duly used as preparation for the eternity. He was at that time, in the spring, 1854, engaged with great preparations for the tremendous war with Russia; and I wrote a document to his ambassador in Washington, showing that if Emperor Napoleon would be truly great in this and in all future ages, and truly happy in all eternity, he instead of preparations for war with Russia, should call all bishops of his Empire to a Latin convention with me in Paris. In that convention my manuscript which I wrote A. D. 1849, in Latin and in which I concentrated the system or the magnetic chain to bind the Dragon, REVEL. xx. 2, who deludes Emperors and Kings to keep people in bondage so that when they break their bonds they are as the wildest beasts killing till they are killed, should be examined and bishops and their theologians should make any objection, but all which they object they must object in writing, to be then annexed to my manuscript and published with my remarks in Latin and in translations, that nations and their ecclesiastical and political representatives might judge, each for himself, whether we have received or not received the commission and the credentials of our mission for the introduction of the promised new era of harmony and peace amongst all nations. A Latin convention for this purpose was first appointed in the City of New-York A. D. 1849, and the Archbishop of Baltimore was urged by our Latin manuscript Epistle and English printed circular, to move the whole synod of bishops who met at that time in Baltimore, to attend our Latin convention, and those who could not attend it themselves to send the most qualified Theologians to attend it. And John Hughes bishop of New-York, was particularly exhorted, that he, as bishop of the place of the convention, was principally bound to bring his Theologians to said convention. But when all my endeavoring to move bishops as well as the government of the United States to send able Latin scholars to attend said convention, did not move them to do so, I translated at length that manuscript into German and into English, and appointed conventions in those languages. But I could not move such as have great influence at the government, to attend those conventions, and then to commence with power the New Era. Therefore I thought, that a trial should be made, whether the United States or the representative of the government of France would comprehend sooner, that nothing in the world could bring greater glory in this life and in all eternity, than the work to examine or order that our message of peace be examined by the best judges of this matter, and be applied for the introduction of the new era. In the hope that Emperor Napoleon would comprehend the great mission which was offered to him in our message, I wrote to his ambassador at Washington, suggesting to the Emperor, that I was ready to come as a citizen of the United States to Paris, to exhibit the credentials which are signs according to prophecies, testifying our mission to move the governments of this world, to establish Christ's peaceable reign or the universal republic of truth and justice, harmony and peace. I expected that the time for the abolition of severe judgments, the principal executor of which is Emperor Napoleon, was expiring.

Not having room in this treatise for any explanation of points which I mention, I show here one of the general tokens, by which the severity of judgments may be measured, to wit, the armies of soldiers, to keep nations in bondage and to defend them against inimical neighbours. The greater in proportion to the number of people, the number of soldiers is, the severer is the judgement. When soldiers shall not be needed, and those who are soldiers, will take up occupations beneficial to mankind, the perfect victory of Christ against the dragon will be celebrated. And if all governments of a christian name would understand to-day our true christian message of peace, they could give directly to those who are soldiers, true christian occupations;

and heathens could be soon converted into true christians. While Emperor Napoleon was gathering together warriors and provisions for the great war against Russia, we offered him the best opportunity to be the first of those who should commence the New Era. Whether he had received from his ambassador in Washington D. C. our offer or not, he may tell for himself; because I have received no answer, although I have offered to the ambassador himself, that although I was ready to go to Paris and show there in our Latin convention to all bishops of the French Empire my mission, which is also the mission of my fellow laborers, and the credentials of our mission, I would visit the ambassador himself and give him as many evidences of this great truth as would be abundantly sufficent for him, to recommend with all his energy our offer to the Emperor, if the ambassador would write to me and call me to Washington. Instead of an answer from the ambassador to my proposition for the true christian triumph of France and for the pacification of the world we have received at length the tremendous answer which has occasioned this my treatise. Here is not the place for an investigation, whether people of "the Latin Race" in Europe and America or others are the principal people who commit the crimes with which citizens of the United States are charged. To the article in the number of the Democrat from which I have quoted some passages, a list of bankruptcies is annexed, which took place in the United States in the years 1857 and 1858. A. D. 1857 the total number of bankruptcies is 4932; and A. D. 1858, 4235. It would be of great consequence, to investigate the deeply secret principal cause of their bankuptcies, and also the native place, education and character of each bankrupt. An impartial examination would bring new contributions to know the secret conspiracy of the servants of his Holiness the apocalystical dragon, to keep nations in bondage.

Emperor Napoleon is not only a spiritualist of the last fashion, but a strong medium of dreadful deluding and destroying demons, and I know much more about his mediumship than he himself and his mediums know about it, and this treatise is written to be prefixed to documents which contain facts that should move all nations of "the Latin race " as well as heretics, to come out from Babylon which is made manifest, in our mission, as a habitation of demons, REVEL. xx. : 2. When I am preparing documents of great warning, servants of demons must send from all quarters of the world testimonies, how the infernal hosts of demons are preparing everywhere their mediums for destruction of human life and property. This and the following treatises are written to deliver other mediums as well as monarchs from the influence of deluding and destroying demons. And Emperor Napoleon should consider this treatise as the most precious Heavenly gift, to bring him and by his instrumentality millions of others into the glorious resurrection. If he studies this book in which this treatise occupies the first place, so as to comprehend it : we have no doubt, that he wlll arrive on our ground and invite us to visit Paris and celebrate there the glorious resurrection of those who belong to " the Latin race" and are yet in their mortal bodies as well as of their departed friends.

In the third of my above mentioned five German volumes is the appearance of Napoleon I. reported, when he was brought on the 24th June, 1839, before me in his materialistic superficial imperial shape. But when I was looking into his interior condition, the awful distress and tremendous darkness blotted out all his imperial splendor. He and others in a similar deceitful condition are influencing the Emperor. But I am writing as his most sincere friend in his behalf and that of nations, and promise to do all in my power according to my mission to assist him, that he might become a blessing to nations and with our assistance pacify the departed Emperor Napoleon and other congenial friends, and draw them into the glorious New Era. The mediumship of Emperor Louis Napoleon was manifest to us in correspondence with many cases of solemn warnings for the imperial court and all other members of " the Latin race " in close connexion with events which happened in our mission at the same time, when those cases surprised the world. Here I mention the solemn execution of the Archbishop of Paris in Saint Stephen's Church by the mediumship of the priest who has been inspired and supported for that work which required more than human strength, from the infernal regions on the day and at the hour of the novena, which were most suitable according to the prophetical Roman Catholic Calendar in correspondence with what we were doing at the same time in our charge under the Heavenly direction, and in correspondence with what Emperor Napoleon was doing at the same time under the direction of deluding and destroying spirits.

In the first three of my above mentioned five German volumes it was shown, that the doings of the Popes of Rome, who are under the inspiration from the inferior regions, were so controlled through the course of centuries by our Heavenly congress, that those amongst the Popes, who had received peculiar rolls in the great drama of the ecclessiastical and political history, had received also corresponding names to their rolls, and numbers corresponding to their names. And we will have also in this book opportunity to mention some instances of that kind. But here we made this remark on account that at the receipt of the report of the solemn murder of the archbishop, we (after having received instruction in different spirit languages which we need in disclosing the mysteries for the promised New Era, and amongst those languages is also the language by numbers,) saw the great unexpected truth, that the Heavenly congress who are with the Lamb, were so controlling the inferior regions of the papal imperial royal demons, that in Paris which is the principal seat of the intrigues connected with the Papal machinations, also Bishops were so counted, that when the number of their succession according to our spirit language was complete in their Novena, amongst them also the number of the Popish Saints as well as the number of Cardinals and the number of Archbishops of Paris corresponded to the celebration of the mystery of the execution, and that Archbishop has been solemnly executed in Saint Stephen's Church, who was in every respect most qualified for the celebration of that mystery, and the infernal executioners have received permission from the Heavenly Congress to effect the execution by their Medium, a priest who became most qualified to be their Medium ; and this happened for a peculiar warning to the Pope, his Cardinals, Archbishops, Bishops and Priests, that they might not wait, till a general destruction of their persons in connexion with their Hierarchy would take place, but that they might come out from Babylon and become with us messengers of the New Era. I wrote an extraordinary treatise disclosing the deep mystery of the Episcopal succession in Paris connected with the solemn execution of the Archbishop in his complete numbers by the inspiration and assistance of destroying demons, using their sacerdotal medium, according to the permission of the Heavenly Congress, for a peculiar warning to the Papal Imperial Royal Hierarchy and the whole "Latin Race." There not being room in this book for publication of that treatise which is preserved amongst others of my manuscripts to be published in due time and in connection with other treatises which need deeper studies to be fully understood than the memorable events which we have selected for this book, we found proper to mention somewhat regarding that execution in peculiar connexion with Emperor Napoleon and the clergy of his empire, that they might open their eyes and stop the infernal fury which has been made manifest in the preaching of the crusade which gave occasion to this our extraordinary treatise.

The position of Napoleon III. to Napoleon I. according to prophecies, cannot be understood except in the magnetic chain of events shown in our system which will be explained in our monthly theological course, which is announced in this book for the introduction of the New Era. Although the Pope of Rome and the Emperor Nopaleon, both may be destroyed at the abolition of systems which they, each in his sphere, represent, notwithstanding this we labour most earnestly, that their lives may be preserved and they come into our New Jerusalem and draw millions of others into it. At the explosion of the percussion shells, in which others have been killed at the entrance to the theatre, but Napoleon's life was preserved, peculiar manifestations took place. The explanation of that mystery will be annexed as an appendix to the above mentioned treatise, in which the mystery of the succession of Bishops of Paris is explained. The representative of bishops who have generated such fruits as are manifest in Paris, has suffered death. But Emperor Napoleon's life was preserved at other occasions of danger as well as at the explosion of the percussion shells; and we are labouring in the expectation that he will understand this book and become with us a great apostle removing the severe judgments and the dreadful bondage, which are connected with his present government, and assisting us in the preparation for the great resurrection of those in their mortal bodies as well as of their departed friends. All that is written in this book is written for a peculiar instruction to all, and especially to those who are strong Mediums ef deluding and destroying spirits the great Prince amongst whom is Emperor Napoleon. But we write this treatise, to deliver him from those miserable tyrants, and to make him a preacher of peace also to his departed friends. What we write for him, we write that it might be used by all readers.

As strange as the point in the inscription, that James Buchanan is according to the merciful Divine Benignty President of the United States, may appear not only to other governments, but also to many big men in these United States, and to millions of others who are deceived by big men, we write to undeceive all, and that also those might be saved, who would have been already destroyed, if instead of James Buchanan Col. Fremont had been elected President of the United States. We are on quite another ground from which we consider human affairs, than that from which they are generally considered: because I speak as Medium of the Heavenly Powers by whom I am sent to draw nations on our ground. For there is no salvation but destruction for them, if they will not arise from their present degraded condition upon our ground from which they will see matters as we see them. In the meantime we instruct them by facts, that they might know, that we are correct and they are in delusion. I am as independent from President Buchanan, as his enemies are, and if he has received my writings which I have sent and directed to him, he did not make use of them; although I suppose that my writings directed to him since his Presedential administration, remain in the hands of others. But in case, he had received and read those my writings, and had despised the course which is shown in our message as the course for redemption of nations from the Papal Imperial Royal and other oppresive and speculating powers, the inscription in regard to him remains true; and when I do not despair of Emperor Napoleon's conversion from his dragon to our Christ, I expect with great confidence, that President Buchanan will be sooner converted than Napoleon; although I do not know, how the Heavenly Congress see this matter, because I am not in their congress but only a medium of messengers sent from that congress. But in every case the inscription to this treatise is true, as the bitterest enemies of President Buchanan may learn from the following items, and by studying this whole book they themselves may be brought upon our ground and assist us in drawing the President upon the same ground for the redemption of nations from all tyrannical powers.

I was in Cincinnati, when honorable James Buchanan was nominated Democratic Candidate for Presidency. That nomination took place on the 6th of June 1856. During the balloting of the Delegates I was inspired, and said on the 4th June, to Doctor B. F. White, that I felt it to be my duty to endeavor to make known to the Delegates our message of Peace and the credentials of our mission, and that the place for that purpose was providentially prepared a few days before that by a building having been removed at the front of Burnet's Hotel, the largest hotel in which the largest portion of the democratic delegates boarded, and I made the proposition to Docter B. F, White, that he should open the meeting for my address. He promised to do so. He was a strong medium of spirits of the so called Republican Party. But I belong to no party, supporting Truth wherever I find it sufficiently proven, and working against delusion and error, wherever I have enough evidence against them. B. F. White knew somewhat in regard to our message, having heard some of my speeches and having read my pamphlet which had been published in Cincinnati a few days before that nomination. We agreed strictly to observe two points; in the first place to say nothing which would have a reference to any party, and to proclaim only, what all should hear regarding our message of Peace. The second point was that we should speak before sunset, aud finish our speeches before night should commence. I was certain about the point which I related to Dr. White, that if we would speak in the night, some disaster would happen during our speeches on that occasion. Dr. White accompanied me, while we were going to the open lot, on which we had agreed to address the Democratic Delegates; but on our way we met with somebody who commenced to talk with Dr. White. I left them talking and went to the spot agreed upon to deliver our address. But while I was waiting more than one hour there, Dr. White did not come. I felt that I alone should notdeliver my message there. He came at length while there was already twilight. I said to him, that it was too late and we should not speak. I assured him again, that I was determined not to speak that night. But he replied that he was determined to speak, and that he was sure, that nothing would happen. But I repeated, that some disaster would happen. Then another strong medium came. He belonged to the same Republican party that Dr. White did, and lived with Dr. White. His spirit confirmed the assertion of the spirit of Dr. White, that nothing would happen, if we would address the Delegates. Then I would not interfere any longer, and Dr. White commenced to address the assembled. While he spoke, the crowd increased and some commenced to make disturbance. At that moment the Editor of the Democratic Review in Washington City interfered, and he took the platform, addressing the audience and saying, that the speaker should not be disturbed, and that he supposed the speaker belonged to the Democratic party. I said once more to Dr. White, that it was high time to leave that place. But he again asserted, that he was certain, that nothing would happen. And the other medium of the Republican party confirmed again Dr White's assertion.

At that moment I left the spot and went to Dr. White's office. Fifteen or twenty minutes after me Dr. White and the other strong medium of deluding and destroying spirits, both came about 9 o'clock P. M. and they were frightened and said, that there was so great a disturbance, that policemen were not sufficient to check it. And they added as a very remarkable instance, that a policeman in trying to check the disturbance, lost his star. But they did not know the other particulars which appeared on the next morning in the newspapers, to wit, that the above mentioned Editor of the Democratic Review in Washington City was dangerously stabbed in his lungs. His wound proved not to be fatal, although it was so large, that when it was sounded, the air which blew out of the wound, extinguished the candlelight which was applied to see the wound. The man who stabbed the Democratic Reviewer from Washington, could not be detected, although the circumstances, from our position considered, make it certain, that he was a medium of distroying spirits belonging to the Republican party. Those spirits were allowed by our leaders to give a prophetical sign. The stabbing took place about 9 o'clock P. M. on the 4th day of June, 1856.

I have circumstantially related the stabbing of the Democratic Reviewer; because from these circumstances in connexion with what follows, it is evident to anybody who understands the prophetic languages by numbers, names and other circumstances, that by that stabbing prophecy has been given under the control of our Heavenly Congress who determined to interfere by our mediumship, that the Democratic party, although they would come in great danger to lose the victory in their battle against the Republican party, would finally conquer their opposition. I was inspired, to give opportunity to that prophecy. Doctor Benjamin Franklin White, a spiritualist and a strong medium of spirits of his party, was the representative of the Republican party; and the Democratic Reviewer from Washington City, was the representative of the Democratic party. Benjamin Franklin White, doctor of medicine, has most suitable names expressing his prophetical position, as we will have perhaps elsewhere opportunity to explain the mystery. As the office of the Democratic Reviewer in Washington was expressive to the mystery of his representation, so were probably his names which I do not keep in memory, and my notes of that time are not at hand, while I am writing this. But the circumstances mentioned in connexion with what we will report on the following pages of this treatise, are superabundantly sufficient to testify, that it was a great prophecy. The delegates then continued their work, till at length on the 6th day of the 6th month James Buchanan was nominated Candidate by Democrats for the Presidential Chair. I looked into the next prophetical almanac which was at hand, and the name of that day was "Benignus." There are Roman Catholic and Protestant calendars which are used by our sphere of spirits in giving prophecies. That was a Protestant almanac; *because* that was a Protestant affair. At the events of great importance names of our prophetical almanacs correspond to the events. *Benignus*, the Latin is in English *Benign*, that is kind or *generous*. From thence we adopted the word *Benignity*, that is *grace* or *graciousness*, *generosity*, *kindness*, in the inscription of this treatise.

If I would explain the prophetical language by numbers and names and other circumstances, this would require more room than our economy could here spare, and we could not consent to publish at this time a much larger volume than manuscript is prepared for this volume, also in case that somebody should be desirous to publish it; because this volume contains more than most readers will be prepared to study and digest thoroughly. Therefore we must delay other manuscripts for other occasions, and we can explain only a little of what we know; because otherwise we could never finish our explanations. But the substance given in the prophecy on the 4th and 6th of June at the nomination of Hon. James Buchanan, in which he became the Democratic Candidate for Presidency, did announce, that

James Buchanan will become President of the United States by the interference of the Heavenly congress of spirits who are commissioned to introduce the Peaceable Reign of Christ or the Universal Republic of truth and justice, harmony and peace, by the instrumentality of messengers whom I represent to move the governments and nations for action to accomplish the great object to which prophecies of all ages and of all nations have their tendency; but notwithstanding that his administration will be for the increase of the 4th Beast in the 7th chap. of Daniel, the number of the name of which is 666, Revel. xiii,

17 and 18, and its fundamental number is 6, and notwithstanding that President Buchanan will continue the administration for the support of that Beast, till he arrives either on our ground or is taken away, nothwithstanding this, he is given as President by the Heavenly Congress in divine mercy, according to the Benignus, or according to the merciful divine Benignity, that a great door for the commencement of the promised peaceable reign of Christ will be opened, which would have been locked for this time, if the opposition had succeeded and brought their Candidate Col. Fremont upon the Presidential Chair.

Nobody should say, that I interpret prophecy after its fulfilment. Any body who has studied the first three of my German volumes, the 3d of which appeared A. D. 1840, if he knew the above mentioned circumstances and had reflected upon them, would have been qualified to interpret the prophecy in Cincinnati on the 6th day of the 6th month 1856, at noon time, while the roaring of the cannon was announcing the nomination of James Buchanan. But whether he will be the great hero, to commence the Millennium in the White House at Washington and proclaim the Millennial glory to other governments on the globe, or whether he will perish in the Beast and its ten Horns, as his predecessors did, and another will obtain and spread the Heavenly blessings offered to President Buchanan, is not expressed in the prophecy. But we write in the expectation, that at length he will comprehend this and act accordingly.

After that great prophecy I thought that my duty was to behave perfectly neutral during the great struggle of the two parties, to wit, the Democratic and the Republican, at the presidential campaign. I delivered then in several places of the State of Ohio public addresses; but I made expressedly everywhere the remark, that I was perfectly independent from all political parties and proclaiming according my mission the message of Peace to all parties and sects, to prepare them for the promised New Era. But after every address, notwithstanding all my protestation, Republicans cried that I belonged to their party, and Democrats were dissatisfied.

At length I arrived in Pittsburgh Pa. and a medium of strong spirit manifestations and public street preacher has offered to me for a present a copy of Fremont's Life published by Horace Greeley & Co.: and made the remark, that if I should read it, I would be moved to act for Fremont's election. I remarked, that I would have in these circumstances scarcely sufficient time to read so much regarding Fremont and also regarding Buchanan, as would be necessary to know both as far as to decide according to my knowledge of both for one or the other; and then it would be against my usual course, if I should take any part in the election of the one or the other. But I took the offered book, and then I was inspired to study it with great attention, and I was astonished, that in the falsely called Republican party the large number of those who are for the Republican against the monarchial cause, could be so duped and deceived by miserable speculators and monarchial agents as to accept Col. Fremont as their Candidate for Presidency. Here is not the place to show by the testimonies which are contained in the book published by Horace Greeley for a recommendation of his Presidential Candidate Fremont, what this man is. The testimonies were not understood by the Republicans who are so obscured by the Papal Imperial Royal magnetism, that although they have eyes, they do not see matters of this kind. I make only the general remark, that the United States would have been already burning in revolutions and wars not for the Republican but for the monarchial cause, if Fremont had been elected President.

After the perusal of that book I read also the book published by Democrats for Buchanan's election. Then I understood that not only the Heavenly congress who do not deprive men of their free will although they control their actions for the final triumph of the true Republican cause, but that also I was in duty bound to enlighten Citizens of Pennsylvania, who had to decide the Presidential election, that they might know Fremont and Buchanan, as they must be known for the welfare of the country. I did it when I had an opportunity. A short time after that I heard a speech of " Hon. Burlingame," which contained a heap of "burlygames," and misrepresentations, deluding and instigating Citizens of Pennsylvania against Buchanan, and soliciting them to vote for Fremont. Then I wrote what I thought proper, that it was used by others, and under the control of our Heavenly leaders good and bad people, those who co-operated in truth with us, without any other interest except the interest of nations, as well as those who co-operated for their private interest, contributed their share for Buchanan's election according to the merciful Divine Benignity, that we could peaceably prepare people for the New Era until this hour under his administration, and warn the inhabitants of the United States, that they should lose no time to avert the impending judgments, which would have already effected a general destruction without hope of escape, except by blind submission to tyrants, if the falsely called Republicans who have been made blind tools of the monarchial speculations, had succeeded with the intrusion of their candidate upon the Presidential Chair. If President Buchanan and the American Nation should continue in their course until the impending general judgments would destroy the country, then also in this most deplorable case, my inscription of this treatise would remain true, and nobody else but the American Nation should be blamed, that they neglected to make use of the divine mercy and the divine benignity, by virtue of which they should have at least during Buchanan's administration until now made use of the precious time, and spread our message for the pacification of the world.

The explanation of the given hints and what is connected with them, would need a large and special volume; but we have mentioned here as much as sufficient, and remark that if Mr. Horace Greeley and Readers of the Tribune, are desirous to know their great hero Col. Fremont, as he is exhibited in my above mentioned treatise, I will extract out of it the passages which belong to him and to the slanderers and abusers of President Buchanan, and send them to be published in the New-York Tribune with such remarks of the Editors as they would think proper to add, under the condition to publish then also my answers to their remarks as I should think proper to make additions for a wholesome instruction to the Editors and Readers of the Tribune, that they might be delivered from the delusion by which the True Republican cause is ruined.

If they are anxious to know truth, they will understand this book and determine to act with us for the redemption of nations from the monarchial Powers. In this case they are requested to write to me under the directions which are given in the proper place of this book, and assure me in their writing, that they accept the proposition, and are determined to co-operate with us for the introduction of the promised New Era of Harmony and Peace, in which Publishers and Editors will have nobler occupations than they have at present in the servitude laboring hard for the support of the Beast and its ten Horns. This was to be mentioned in this connection in regard to Hon. Horace Greeley and the New-York Tribune. But the parties of the so-called Republicans and Abolitionists will receive in an other treatise of this book extraordinary lessons, that they might at length commence to co-operate with us for the introduction of the Millennial glory. Many of them have abused and misrepresented me in my mission. Therefore I do not marvel that they have abused and misrepresented also President Buchanan not only during the campaign, but also during his administration. We have made urgent appeals to him, to make use of our message against the enemies of this Republic; but he has neglected to do so, or perhaps my documents did not reach himself, or the neglect must be attributed rather to his enemies than to him. They would not hear me, and probably they would not have heard him. Matters have to come so far as they are made manifest in this book. After the Crusade of professed Monarchists in Europe became as manifest, as there is the Crusade of Abolitionists and false Republicans against him manifest in America, we expect that President Buchanan will comprehend at length our mission, and endeavor to arrive upon our ground to become the great Apostle of the New Era. If he comprehends this book and makes use of our weapons of the spirit, he will be a partaker of the great promise, and he will convert millions of his enemies of all parties and sects into his true friends, and those who will not be converted, will be destroyed. Moses and other Prophets of the Old Testament, Christ and his Apostles and Prophets through the course of centuries of the Christian Era as well as of this time, have testified our mission, and signs are continuously repeated, announcing the final victory of the cause entrusted to our mission, as those who will study this book thoroughly, will be convinced of this unexpected assertion. But here for the close of this treatise we remark for the peculiar use to President Buchanan and others who are invited to become our fellow laborers in the true Republican or true Christian against the Monarchial or Antichristian cause, that in the second and third chapters of the REVELATION the seven churches are typical symbols of the seven states of the church, and that to one or the other of these states each church of the christian name can be reduced, from the time the Revelation has been published, to the time in which Christ comes or is made manifest by our mission, in which that is performed and disclosed, which is needed for his peaceable reign on earth.

In the second chapter of the REVELATION, verses 18 to 29 is Thyatira the type of the Roman Catholic Church. In the 24th and 25th verses to those Roman Catholics "who have not known the depths of Satan," who has brought them so on the surface and perverted the truth of the doctrine, that they keep the shadow for truth, it is said: "I will put upon you none other burden. But that which ye have, hold fast till I come," REVEL. ii: 24 and 25. They have to keep the heavy burden of ceremonies, feasts and fasts, and all kinds of other practices which are not proficient to intellectual and moral perfetion of man, although they are connected with enormous expenses for the support of Priests and many others, and for all the buildings, vessels, and all kinds of instruments, not knowing what is in their depth, till Christ comes. And then it is said; "and he that overcometh and keeps my works unto the end, to him will I give power over the nations: and he shall rule them with a rod of iron; as the vessels of a potter shall they be broken to shivers: even as I received of my Father. And will I give him the morning star," REVEL. ii: 26, 27 and 28.

Here in the quoted verses at Christ's coming Christ's relation to him who overcometh, is such as the relation of a father to his son, who inherits from the father all things which the father possesses. Christ has not been known in the churches of Babylon, as he is made known in our mission to introduce the New Jerusalem. Christ in his appearance in flesh was the Head, that is the representative of his body of followers; but they could not establish his peaceable reign. It was necessary, that through the course of centuries matters should be so developed, as Prophets of the Bible as well as in the subsequent ages did prophesy; and I, to be qualified for my present mission, had to go not only through the usual studies of the Roman Catholic Church, but I had also to study continuously, with all sincerity of my heart, the sources of human knowledge and the investigations of different parties and sects, to support the Roman Catholic Church against the assaults of her adversaries, and was found qualified to be public Imperial Royal Professor of Bibical Literature in that Church. In the charge of my Professorship I considered myself peculiarly bound to defend with the use of the Bible that church against all aggressions of the adversaries. I did not know at that time, that the spirit of my Lord was preparing me through all stages of my life for my present office. But while I was investigating the depth of the "burden," of that church, comparing it with the Jewish and Heathen antiquities and with the developement of the mysteries of those antiquities through the centuries of the christian Era, when I was duly prepared and the time of the last development of preparations for the Millennial glory arrived, I was called by messengers of the Heavenly Congress to "the works," which were to be performed and explained by my instrumentality, and, under the direction of Heavenly leaders, who were most qualified to be my leaders in "those works," I overcame all difficulties and I kept the "works of my spiritual Father Jesus Christ unto the end," until all has been performed and explained, that belongs to the commencement of the Millennial glory, or what is the same, for the New Era or the New Jerusalem.

And we, that is, the whole body of messengers whom I represent, have received "the iron rod and the morning star," the two symbols of our mission. The first symbol testifies, that nations which reject our message of Peace, will be broken to pieces. We do not break them, but we announce to them judgments by which they will be broken. But we are laboring to save nations, that they as god's people might come out from Babylon, that they be not partakers of her sins and receive not of her plagues, REVEL, xviii : 4. If people hear our voice, they will be partakers of the Heavenly blessings prepared for them in the New Era or in the New Jerusalem, and while they will be saved, their political and ecclesiastical systems "as the vessels of a potter will be broken to shivers." Systems that could not bring better fruits than those which the political and ecclesiastical history and the experience of our days shows, are founded in delusion and deception, which were generating continuous destruction of human life and property and all the misery which is founded in political and ecclesiastical follies. But enlightened men and women of all ages and amongst all nations have seen a new day, and to us has been entrusted "the Morning Star," the symbol testifying that we have received all that is needed for the new day, the New Era, which our morning star is announcing.

All my published works and all my manuscripts are testifying, that it is impossible to save this country from the yoke of monarchs and from the most abject degradation and servitude, by any weapons except those which have been entrusted to our charge by Christ's spirit. And those who study this whole book from the commencement to the end, in the same order in which the documents are placed in it, so that they understand each portion separately and the connection of it with all that precedes, to be prepared for the right understanding of what follows, to comprehend at length the whole, will be as convinced as I am, that we, that is I and all my visible and invisible fellow laborers, have truly received the great commission to move nations for the introduction of the promised New Era, which will be the universal Republic of Truth and Justice, Harmony and Peace amongst all nations, the Dispensation of the Fulness of Times, in which all in

Heaven and on Earth will be gathered together in Christ, Ephes, 1 : 10.

Readers must keep in mind, that all that is written in this book is only a preparation to the "monthly theological course" which is appointed at the end. In the "monthly course" the system or the chain to bind the Dragon REVEL. xx : 2 will be explained and that will be made manifest, which is mentioned in this book but cannot be explained. And our proceedings in that monthly course will be then published in different languages for a testimony to all nations, to move them for co-operation, that all in Heaven and on Earth might be brought to Harmony and Peace.

President Buchanan! allow me to close this treatise with some important words to you! For you we need no more testimonies than those partly printed partly written documents which I have sent at different critical occasions by the mail directly to you, if they had been handed to you, and you had studied them with such attention, as they deserved to be studied by the President of the United States. Those testimonies would have been sufficient to convince you, that no other weapons can be used for the victory against your enemies and the enemies of the true Republican cause, by whom this country is overflowed, and who in Europe are preaching crusades against you and the supporters of the cause entrusted to your care, except the weapons of Christ's spirit entrusted to our care. Those who are with the Lamb, called, chosen and faithful, will overcome the Beast and its ten Horns. REVEL, xvii : 14. This will not take place with preparations for war and with armies of soldiers; but we have the Heavenly armies upon white horses, REVEL xix : 14, and offer to all our enemies reconciliation with Heaven and temporal and eternal most precious blessings. But if they reject the Heavenly gifts, all infernal hosts are subject to our Heavenly armies, and by these executioners of divine judgments as many of our enemies will be destroyed as sufficient, to move the rest of them to repentance. Although I could give thousands of instances of destruction of enemies of our cause, who have been cast into the inferior regions, because they have rejected the Heavenly gifts offered them by our instrumentality, I will mention only one instance for a peculiar warming to you.

A. D. 1849 at our appointment of a Latin convention in the City of New-York for an examination of the magnetic chain shown by our instrumentality to bind the Dragon, REVFL XX: 2, I sent to President Zach. Taylor a copy of my printed English circular in which that convention was appointed, and a copy of my large Latin letter, taken from the copy which was directed and sent to the Archbishop of Baltimore to be read to all Bishops of the United States, who were at that time assembling their Synod in Baltimore. To those copies I added my English letter in which I addressed President Taylor showing to him, that our message is as important for all political as for all ecclesiastical governments and especially for the government of the United States to stop the Papal Imperal Royal or monarchial influence and to restore the true Republican cause, and that therefore he, President Zach. Taylor, was in duty bound to send to said convention qualified Latin scholars to attend it. In my printed and written documents as many items have been concentrated as would have been sufficient to move the President to do what was required, if President Taylor had been qualifyed for his post. We have warned him most solemnly, that he as the twelfth President, should not be a traitor of the Republican cause, as Judas Jscariot was a traitor of Christ's cause. But my warnings were not regarded by President Taylor.

After the destruction of the armies of those who were deceived in Europe by their leaders that they were fighting with carnal weapons for the Republican cause, I wrote again to President Taylor showing, that he was responsible for all destruction of human life and property, which would have been saved, if he had not neglected to fulfil his highest duty which has been shown to him in my documents; but that, notwithstanding this, according to divine mercy, to save him and by his instrumentality many others, I was again authorized to apply to him and to show, what he ought to do in those circumstances, to open the way for spreading our message of Peace amongst all nations. But when all my efforts to move the President for an energetic action for the support of the true Republican cause remained without effect, I committed him to the judgment of the Heavenly Congress.

On the 9th day of July, 1850, at 5 o'clock A. M., shortly

after my arrival in Cleveland Ohio, an Angel of the Lord, a holy martyr, came to me and said, that I should write directly to the Congress and show that President Taylor had neglected to fulfil his highest duty and deserves on this account the severest judgment. After having finished my writing on that day, I was looking to find in Cleveland somebody acquainted with a congressman to whom we could entrust my document. But on that day I could not find such a man. On the 10th I went to a "free soil" minister with the expectation, that he might know such a man. That minister was not at home; but his wife said, that he had gone to the Post Office and was soon expected to return. He returned with the message, that President Taylor died at 10 o'clock P. M. of the preceding night. Then I understood the mystery, that my writing was not prepared for the Congress of the United States in Washington but for the Heavenly Congress, and I have shown to that minister my writing directed to the Congress of the United States. I did not hear before, that the President had been taken sick, although I have heard afterwards, that his sickness was very short, and that his last words were, that he was departing with the consciousness, that he had fulfilled his duties. This is the consolation which ministers of darkness impart to such destroyers as General and President Zach. Taylor was. If he had had any regard for the lives of his fellow beings and for their true happiness, he would have understood my documents and have done what was his duty for the destruction of the Beast, its image and the false prophet, which destroy every year an enormous amount of human life and property.

Although I have mentioned in this treatise several strange facts, some of the following will appear more strange; but they will be the more comprehended, the more this whole book shall be understood. Not only the order which I received in the morning of the day on which Zach. Taylor departed, to write to the congress that he had neglected to fulfill his highest duty, but also the day and hour, in which he daparted, were most suitable for the celebration of the mystery of Zach. Taylor's death, and the tremendous fire in Philadelphia at 4 o'clock P. M. or 6 hours before Taylor's death, was a prophetical precursor of his death. In that fire a number of persons were killed by a terrible powder explosion commemorating the fact that the privileged murderer had been nominated President in that city. All that happened by the dreadful influence of infernal demons under the control of messengers from our congress, who have given at the exact hours on the proper day signs of a great warning. As soon as I heard of President Taylor's death, I understood, that I was ordered to write to the Heavenly Congress of the United States, that is, the congress of the holy prophets and martyrs, who have the commission to unite finally all states of all governments on the globe in Christ's peaceable reign or the universal Republic of Truth and Justice, according to the prophecies which have been given by their mediumship, while they were yet in their mortal bodies. My writing to the congress was copied by one of our departed messengers, and when President Taylor departed, my writing was shown to him. Such things would not appear strange to Bible readers, if they would understand what they read. Here is no room to explain the actions of the departed, amongst which there is also writing and reading. When the departed President was reading my document showing that he had neglected to fulfil his highest duty, his animal passion of murder was aroused, to kill the writer. That privilege was granted to him only under the condition, if he succeeds by taking a toad in possession, and by its instrumentality, poisoning the water of the well at the house in which I used to stop. The water was poisoned ; the prophetess and her husband with whom I boarded, when I was in that section of the country, were by drinking the water, taken sick, and they recovered as soon as they ceased to use the water, but they could not catch the toad. It happened before my arrival with them. And when I arrived in their house and would drink of that excellent water, they warned me. But I did not care about their warning and drank, and was straightway taken sick and continued to be sick, till a Heavenly messenger came at the right hour and took the sickness away. At length the toad was caught and killed the right day and hour by the husband of the prophetess, who was a zealous Democrat. He was in many battles with Generals of Napoleon I. and killed men and animals ; but he assured us oftentimes, that he never had so much trouble in killing any creature, as with that toad, and never heard so pitiful lamentations as have been poured out by that toad when it was dying. Zach. Taylor, when he was compelled to leave the toad and to enter into the infernal regions of his inner life, into his torments, resisted as long as he could ; but when the right day and hour came, he could not resist longer. If you study this whole book so, as you need to study it, you will not be surprised at such unexpected events. You read in the fifth chapter of Mark, that a whole legion of demons, that is a whole regiment of soldiers who have been destroyed in a battle, have been permitted to enter into a heard of hogs. But they could not remain there, and were compelled to enter into the depth of the lake. And General Taylor who had destroyed many people, after having despised reconciliation and apostleship offered to him by virtue of our mission, was at length not allowed to be with a toad, but was compelled to descend into the abyss.

I have given here only some hints of strange events which are in connection with other events which could not be mentioned here, nor can we explain what we have mentioned without enlarging this treatise. But we have written a peculiar treatise in which President Taylor's spirit manifestation by the instrumentality of a toad is circumstantially explained in a manuscript which will be published when required. But here we have mentioned as much as we could in this confined space, and we hope, that not only you, President Buchanan, but also Emperor Napoleon as well as your friends and enemies in general will reflect upon such things with earnestness.

On the 24th day of June 1839, I retnrned from Philadelphia to Boston with many collections to write the third of my five German volumes, and to show, that the memorable events which have been reported in my first and second volumes, happened according to prophecies, as signs testifying our mission. When, on that day, as is reported in my 3d volume, I was praying in my room and preparing to write the 3d volume, Emperor Napoleon, in his Imperial splendour stood before me with the invitation, that I might become his medium. I looked into his inner state, and the magnetic outward splendor disappeared, and his inner wretchedness and distress were manifest, and he could not stand any longer before me, and, with an explosion like a powerful thunderclap, he left me and took the direction to Europe. The title of my third volume, if we translate it from German into English, reads :

" Memorable events in the life of Andrew Bernardus Smolnikar. Third volume containing the Explanation of Prophecies, by which Christ the Lord, has confirmed that he has appeared unto us for the fulfilling of his promises, in order to restore his reign upon the whole earth and to give his peace to all nations, and has at his appearance appointed the author as an extraordinary messenger, and performed by him all the mysteries for the foundation of that peace &c., New-York, 1840."

We read, " Put on the whole armour of God, that ye may be able to stand against the wiles of the devil. For we wrestle not against flesh and blood, but against principalities, against the rulers of the darkness of this world, against spiritual wickednes in high places." EPHES. vi : 11 and 12. These are the secret enemies whom we must know, and we must stand on a ground, on which they cannot come, and from which we will conquer them. When Napoleon was allowed to approach me with the invitation, that I should follow him, that is, that I should become his medium, he was allowed in a like manner, as the tempter or devil in the 4th chapter of MATTHEW was allowed to tempt Jesus. Napoleon was one of the dragons or devils, who was permitted to do so for a great instruction to all rulers on the globe. There is not one, but there are many dragons or devils, leading each his sphere of infernal demons or degraded departed spirits. You will understand the more the mystery, the farther you proceed in studying this book. Now is renewed and fulfilled, what is written in the gospels, and what in the Bible was not understood, receives light by our experience. Jesus could not descend from his height, to become a medium of one of these rulers of darkness. And likewise I could not do this. This dragon, this spirit of delusion and destruction, when I commenced to look into his interiors was made manifest, and he could not stand any longer. He was compelled to leave me instantly and to be tormented seeking another medium. At lenghth, because our message of Peace has been rejected and people were so degraded, that the European Revolution of 1848 opened the way to the throne of Napoleon III, Napoleon I. could have this as a suitable medium to delude and destroy nations. And to this dragon so much of human life and property has been sacrificed, that for the celebration of the birth of the Papal Imperial Royal Mary on the 8th September 1855, thirty thousand soldiers have been murdered at the taking of Sebastopol. Nobody who does not see human affairs from our position, can duly appreciate the criminality of such a tremendous madness, from which to deliver Napoleon III. and his armies, you, President Buchanan, are able to give us a powerful assistance. I do not despair of the conversion of Napoleon III himself. When people descend so deep into the society of infernal spirits that there is no other remedy than destruction of many to save the remnant, then according to divine judgment people receive such rulers as are connected with one or the other of the infernal dragons, to inspire them with the infernal furies to destroy each other. Great warriors are great mediums of the princes of darkness. But if they are reached by our instrumentality, they when they are studying our message of Peace, are drawing their leading spirits from their depth of misery into a better condition. Napoleon III. if he could be moved to study our message of Peace and to act accordingly, could reach his uncle Napoleon, and draw him into the pacification. What we mention here, is explained in our system for the promised New Era.

This is the joyful message, which is to be communicated by your instrumentality, President Buchanan, to Emperor Napoleon and other monarchs, that they might study our message of Peace and become our fellow laborers to draw their living and departed friends into the New Era, or the New Jerusalem, which is to be introduced by our instrumentality. And you, President Buchanan, are powerfully exhorted, to prepare for the Kingdom of our Lord and his Christ, REVEL. xi: 15. Editors and translators of the New Testament were so ignorant of the true Christian principles that they took instead of "the kingdom of our Lord and his Christ" the wrong reading "the kingdoms" in plural number; but there will be one kingdom, that is, one government of our Lord and his Christ. And this will be a true Republican government—to give explanations about which there is no room here, but we remark, that this great truth will become self-evident to those who comprehend this book. And we expect, that you, respected President Buchanan, will comprehend it and then you will take the spiritual weapons, which are comprehended in our message, for the conversion of monarchs into true republicans, which is the same, as true christians. But in the first place bishops and priests in America are to be moved, to attend our monthly theological course and then assist us at the conversion of monarchs. And we expect that by your good example and your assistance bishops and priests will learn at length to comprehend their highest duty. Matters come to maturity; but we will not expatiate, because we have already extended this treatise so far: nothing but our duty to do all in our power for the pacification of nations, moved us to write it according to our mission for the redemption of oppressed humanity.

Postscript to the first treatise. I arrived the last time in Washington City at the end of March, this year, 1859, and remained there until the 8th of April. Then I walked to Baltimore and wrote to hon. Hicks, Governor of Maryland, and invited him, to study the documents which I had offered to President Buchanan, but he had no time to study them, although they contain matters of great importance for all governments to remove War and establish Peace on the whole globe. I mentioned many items in my letter that I expected to move the Governor to accept my offer; but, received no answer. The same time a great sign was given so that I was sent speedily from Baltimore to the Western Reserve of Ohio. At my arrival there the Spring was changed in a severe Winter, and I commenced to write during a great storm and snow on Easter Saturday, April 23d 1859, a new treatise exhibiting wonders and signs in connexion with Presidents and other high Officers of the Federal Government of the United States and showing, how they are subjugated by the Beast with seven Heads and are supporting the ten Horns of that Beast, and that there will be a great destruction of human life and property in this country, as there is in Europe, if it shall not be stopped by receiving and spreading our Heavenly message of Peace, which is developed by our mediumship. Since my public appearance in my present mission there was continuous correspondence of memorable events connected with the Government of the United States and memorable events connected with the steps of my mission, containing most solemn warnings to this Government, and many striking instances are concentrated in said treatise which was intended to occupy the second place in this book. But we found that the book would become too large, to be bought and studied by many who might be attracted to study this and then to co-operate with us for the fulfilment of the prophecy which was given by the disappearance of the Steamboat President and all persons, who were in it at the same time in which President Harrison died in such connexion with what was set in type at the same time for my 4th volume, entitled: "The one thing Needfull," and with the documents which were at the same time sent from Europe for our use, and explained in said volume in such correspondence with the disappearance of the Steamboat President and the death of President Harrisson, that the prophecy contained in those events is manifest, by which the spirit assures us, that he will sweep away the antichristian government of the United States as well as other governments. Knowing this, people of the United States and their Officers may avoid all the dreadful destruction, which is in Europe preparing the way, that at length governments and people will pay attention to our message and learn how to establish perfect peace on the whole globe.

After the disappearance of President Harrison and of the prophetical Steamboat President, solemn warnings were repeated under all following Presidents in correspondence with what happened in our mission; and in this respect President Buchanan is peculiarly remarkable, and in said treatise memorable events of great warnings connected with his administration have been explained. But we must delay their publication, and every reader will find in the following treatises of this book superabundance of solemn warnings, that all might become our zealous fellow laborers for the accomplishment of the glorious promises, and that especially President Buchanan might give to others good example and come from patching the old house which must crumble to pieces, in our peace union and give powerful assistance for the introduction of the promised New Era. Great mercy was shown through him to the country while he is yet in Babylon, but was quenching the fire which would have consumed the country, if his antagonist had been elected President. Therefore, notwithstanding his having neglected the one thing needful until this hour we expect, that he will arrive at length on our ground and co-operate with us in building the New Jerusalem.

This treatise, to which I add this postscript June 22d 1859, was written in February last, and the tremendous war and destruction in Italy broke out two or three months afterwards, axactly while I was explaining the thrilling prophecy given by Daniel or Judgement of God performed by Sickles under the control of our Leader in the 14th verse of the 14th chap. of the Revel., "having in his hand a sharp sickle." He gave to the dostroying Spirit the permission to seize the medium and to show prophetically what he will do in hundreds of thousands of cases, if the right order shown in our Plan, will not be restored. There is a depth in the mystery of the unexpected tragedy, in which all actors have most suitable names and offices, each for the post he occupies; and the most suitable spot as well as the most suitable day and hour were selected for the performance, with all the preceding, accompanying and following circumstances in correspondence with our doing on the same Sunday Sexagesima on which this year the tragedy was perpetrated, as well as what happened in the preceding years since my first public appearance in my present mission on that Sunday A. D. 1838, and the initiation which has been imparted to me on that Sunday for my present ministry, by the martyr on the white cloud, who has in his hand a sharp sickle, Revel. xiv. 14. I give here only some hints; but the explanation is given in connexion with many other cases of a great warning to this government in the treatise, the publication of which must be delayed; for we expect that the contents of the following treatises of this book will be strong enough to awaken the enemies of President Buchanan to give us assistance to awaken him from his lethargy, if he should not be sooner aroused to assist us to deliver them from their wrong course, by which they injure the great cause of the true Freedom of nations.

In the great ignorance in which people are regarding the inner life of man and the spirit world, they are reading many signs of the times, without understanding what they read.

I mentioned above, that I started on the 8th April from Washington. It is to be understood that so many signs and wonders took place and so many secrets were disclosed, while I was trying spirits in Washington, that a book of this size would be too small to comprehend them. On the 8th April 1859, I finished all work which I had to perform in Washington, at the same hour, in which four men were, all at once in Baltimore, hung by the neck, till dead, although the black struggled some minutes longer with death than his white companions. As soon as my work was finished in Washington, I started and walked to Baltimore, and arrived in that city on the 9th April, when all newspapers were filled with reports of the execution, and with biographies of the executed. I had to read the reports of that execution which belongs to the links of the chain to bind the dragon Revel xx., 2. That reading occasioned my above mentioned letter to governor Hicks. I thought, that perhaps after the execution of some champions of his party, he and other leaders of that party might be more prepared to receive lessons from us, than they were prepared in former times, while I was applying to them in Baltimore, Annapolis, and in hundreds of other cities and villages, exhorting and warning them, to study our message of Peace, and co-operate with us for the true American, or, what is the same, the true Republican cause. But they have despised our warnings. At length matters arrived so far that, if all other warnings of this book should not be sufficient, we expect that the spirit manifestations which are connected with that execution and are mentioned in the fourth treatise of this book, will move them to become our worthy fellow labourers for the fulfilment of the grandest promises. But we repeat, that every reader should study this book in the same order in which it is written, weighing with great attention and earnestness every sentence, till he understands it and retains in his mind all that preceded. If you have studied in this manner this treatise, you are prepared for studying the second treatise.

SECOND TREATISE.

Memorable events, by which the parties of Abolitionists and Republicans as well as subjects of Monarchs should be aroused for co-operation with us, to draw not only the President and the Congress of the United States but also monarchs on our ground for the introduction of the promised universal Republic of Harmony and Peace on earth.

As strange as our disclosures made in the first treatise may appear to those who have neglected to observe the signs of the times, they should not be surprised who know that the time for the fulfilment of the great promises in regard to mankind had arrived, although all things seem to run in quite another course than they expected.

In the 6th verse of the 14th chap. of the REVELS. the first of the three Angels spoken of in that and the following verses, commences to deliver his message. At the commencement of the last century it was known amongst German theologians, that those three angels or messengers are the three men, each of whom is representing a body of messengers by whom the contents of the prophecy given to each of those angels are to be fulfilled. The first is preaching the everlasting Gospel the contents of which are given in the 7th verse. Gospel is Greek evangelion and means glad tidings. The contents of the glad tiding of his preaching is that nations should be converted from their idols to God the creator of the universe, and he announces that the time of judgment had arrived. The commencement of this preaching took place with Martin Luther, so that he is to be considered as the representative of those, who are comprehended in the prophecy of the first of those three angels. But Luther and other preachers who came at that time and afterwards against the Pope of Rome, and continue yet in the same spirit their work, did not know in Luther's time nor afterwards, nor do they know in our time their position, except as they learn it by what is disclosed by the third angel or messenger, who commences his prophecy in the 9th verse of the 14th chap. of the REVEL. In the third of my five German volumes, published from A. D. 1838 to 1842 it has been shown that Luther had a prophetical position, that is, he was according to the term adopted by modern spiritualists, a very strong medium, inspired and supported by his leaders, who were deluding and destroying spirits, who did not know the true God and his Christ, but were prophesying judgments which took place and continue till people shall be converted from their idols to the living God. The three hundred years from Luther's appearance to our appearance, were years of manifold developments preparatory to our mission. Although Luther was born in Eisleben, that means "the life in ice," because the fire of christian charity has been extinguished, and the spirit of persecution was nourished amongst all parties and sects, notwithstanding this great preparations have taken place since his public appearance till our public appearance, and there is an admirable correspondence between his actions in the sixteenth century and my actions which took place in the same years of the nineteenth century, till Luther died on the 18th day of February 1546, which year in our century, I mean 1846, was the great tropical year for dreadful renovations of judgments, for the reason that the leaders of parties and sects and their followers have rejected our message, which I commenced to proclaim after having been publicly initiated to my present mission on the 18th day of February 1838. We shall speak further on in this book regarding the great event. But we have mentioned Doctor Martin Luther as representing the champions of Protestantism against Popery. Their mission is only prophetical. On their position they are supporting Popery or Monarchy in general and they are particularly supporting a number of Popish tenets regarding the Bible, regarding Christ and his mission and manifold other doctrines, in which when they endeavored to improve, they generally apostatized farther from truth towards materialism, than the papal Hierarchy themselves; but they were continuously repeating the substance of their prophecy, that people should be converted from their idols to the living God. But by all that repetition parties and sects multiplied, and there has been since Martin Luther's appearance until this hour so dreadful a Babylon, or confusion and delusion in social, political and ecclesiastical affairs, as there never was before. And while pious men were looking into the prophecies, to see the end of this dreadful Babylon, Doctor Bengel of Wurtemberg in Germany was awakened in the first part of the last century, to compare for many years the prophetical dates of the Revelation with events of the ecclesiastical history, and has shown in his book, entitled : "Erklaerte Offenbarung," which means "Revelation explained," that Christ's manifestation for overcoming his enemies and establishing his peaceable reign on earth, would take place about the year 1836. John Wesley was not the author but only the copy holder of what Doctor Bengel has explained in the Revelation.

That Doctor Bengel was the 2nd angel representing the body of messengers spoken of in REVELATION xiv. 8, has been shown in my above mentioned 3d volume, in which it is made manifest, that the mission of the 2nd angel is as well prophetical, as the mission of the first angel, REVEL. xiv. 6. But in this treatise we had only to mention matters, which have been explained in my quoted volume. Doctor Bengel and the whole body of messengers who came from his school proclaiming the coming of Christ about the year 1836, and Wm. Miller and the army of preachers with him who were proclaiming Christ's coming about the year 1843, and others proclaiming it in some other period, were ignorant about the manner of his coming or of his manifestation for establishing his peaceable reign. All these and many other things have been reserved to the 3d angel or messenger, spoken of in REVEL. XIV. 9. This is our mission. The martyr on the white cloud in the 14th verse, having "in his hand a sharp Sickle," was my leader in what I had to perform in the Roman Catholic Church in the year 1838 as the 3d angel REVEL : XIV. 9. representing the body of messengers, by whom the proclamation of the contents of REVEL : XIV. 9, 10, 11, must be made everywhere. And those great events and the prophecies in which they have been predicted, have been explained in the first three of my above mentioned German volumes; and we have so many credentials or signs according to prophecies testifying our mission, that while we were writing the fifth of my above mentioned five volumes, we were repeating, that sensible readers of those volumes were aware, that five hundred volumes could be written, testifying our mission. And when they study this whole volume and comprehend it, they will be convinced of the same truth.

The third angel or the messenger representing the body of messengers, by whose efficacy the beast and its image and the false prophet supporting them, will disappear from the globe, gives in the last treatise of this book the plan according to which the beast and its image and the false prophet will disappear and Christ's peaceable reign will be established on the whole globe. Peace would have been already established amongst nations of the christian name and they would have labored at this time powerfully in the conversion of Heathens not to one or the other sect but into the peaceable reign of Christ, which will be the universal Republic of Truth and Justice, if those who have been exhorted first, to study our message of peace had fulfilled their highest duty. The first who have been powerfully urged to study our message of peace and the credentials of our mission, were bishops, doctors of divinity and other clergymen of all parties and sects where I had opportunity to reach them. But when they refused to fulfill their highest duty, I was particularly engaged to move abolitionists to study what has been providentially prepared by our instrumentality to move slaveholders themselves for co-operation with us to introduce the millennium or the universel Republic of Truth and Justice and Peace amongst all nations: because I was certain, that if the abolitionists would study it, slaveholders themselves would do the same. But alas! when Jesus was explaining the dreadful condition of Jerusalem, the Jews did not see it. Likewise also citizens of the United States do not see theirs as we see it from the position of our mission. The principal elements of the vulcano the eruption of which is yet latent, are in leaders of abolitionists, who are obstinate materialists refusing to make use of the means which are offered them in our message to extinguish the burning vulcano. They have lost discernment and judgment, when it is most necessary to make the right use of it, to liberate the country from the yoke of tyrants. Although I could write volumes to illustrate my assertion, at this occasion I mention only a little of my experience in the Convention to overcome evil with good, and which was in the newspapers announced under the specious title : Philanthropic Convention to overcome evil with good,and which was held on the 10th, 11th and 12th days of September, 1858, in Utica of the State of New-York. The most influential persons in that Convention were Abolitionists of the Garrisonian and Gerrit Smith's parties and Spiritulists belonging to those and to the Republican party. I attended that Convention to offer the remedy against the pernicious effects, which are produced by the wrong course which leaders of those parties pursue for destruction of this Republic, and to show the course which all true reformers have to pursue for Harmony and Peace of all nations.

That those who are concerned and their followers might be converted to the true Republican cause, and all true Republicans might be strengthened not to be deceived by secret and open servants of tyrants and by deluding and destroying spirits and sectarian ministers of darkness, I find proper to insert here the article which I wrote shortly after the Convention, but I did not find a chance to publish; because we are not popular, when we dare to express so great truths as are comprehended in said lengthy article which reads as follows;

Preparations for the resolutions "to overcome evil with good;" also: introductory remarks to expose the league by which the Utica "Philantrophic Convention" was governed.

There are many such pretenders as the Garrisonian Liberator of Boston, who, under the specious pretext to liberate slaves, are the greatest supporters of slavery, by rejecting the means providentially prepared for deliverance of all men and women from the yoke of tyrants, and by instigating people to Revolutions and other sacrilegious enterprises to ruin this country and bring it under the yoke of monarchs. While I was endeavoring in many places, to move people to study our disclosures regarding the divine plan for a peaceful abolition of all kinds of slavery by co-operation of slaveholders themselves, and for the introduction of the promised universal Republic of Harmony and Peace, which is usually although improperly called the millennium, I found them everywhere so deluded by the infernal league, that they have neglected to study " the one thing needfull " for the true freedom of all nations.

During my travelling in more than twenty of the United States I stopped several times in the Western Reserve of Ohio. I found more worshippers of the Garrisonian Liberator there than in other sections of the country of the same population, those places excepted, which are inhabited by that sect of Quakers who are called " Progressive Friends," who are progressing very fast in the arts of the infernal league for the ruin of the true Republican cause. I arrived A. D. 1847 at the Quaker settlement, called Green Plane, near Xenia in Ohio, and appointed there in a Wesleyan meeting-house a Convention, in which I proposed to explain the signs of our mission and the plan according to which, when it will be understood and spread on the globe, all kinds of slavery will be abolished. I expected that Quakers and other Abolitionists of that section of the country would take great interest in our movement. But I experienced afterwards, that the small Popes of that section were against it, although they themselves did not disturb our Convention; but a Quaker and a Wesleyan minister, both from a distance, were so great disturbers of it , that whenever an important point was to be examined, they directed the attention of the audience to other subjects; although that Convention has been called for an examination of the points concentrated in my manuscript. When I saw, that they were in conspiracy with others in the Convention, I myself dissolved it. I asked then the Quaker preacher Joseph Dugdale, whose residence was next to the meeting-house of the Convention, why he did not attend it. He answered, that he received from the spirit what he needed. I started from thence for the Western Reserve of Ohio, and appointed in

Trumbol Connty a Convention, and sent an article to the Garrisonian Liberator. In that article I assured the Abolitionists, that from my documents which should be examined in the Convention, it would be evident, that we have received the mission, and that we have as credentials of our mission a long chain of signs according to prophecies, by which we are assured, that we will abolish all kinds of slavery and monarchy by the power of the spirit, with the assistance of slaveholders themselves, when abolitionists shall comprehend our message and spread it on the globe.

Lloyd Garrison, the head medium of the infernal league, has published my article, but with such editorial remarks, as were quite agreeable to his master, the infernal Holiness. I forgot to inquire, whether my article appeared or not in the Liberator, till on the first day of our Convention a man remarked that our Convention was small on account of Garrison's editorial remarks to my article and his grand tent meeting in the neighborhood at the same time with our Convention. I came from a distance, and was ignorant of the great provisions made by the infernal holiness to retain his slaves in bondage at the appointment of our Convention for their deliverance. The same man had a copy of the Liberator containing my article with Garrison's remarks. They were read to the Convention. Then I made my remaks and the proposition, to finish our Convention so as to reach on the last day Garrsion's grand tent meeting in Lima, Ohio, and proclaim there our resolutions.

We did so. A committee from our convention went with me, and we arrived in Lima at the Garrisonian tent meeting on the last day. Several thousand persons were assembled, and the first business after our arrival was the reading of a resolution, in which Garrison and his fellow laborers were declared as the true ministers of the Gospel, in connexsion with a fatal blow to the ministers of other sects. A general reception of the resolution was testified with "yes" from a thousand voices; but when the contrary vote was required, there was only my "no" heard; but it was so strong, that it surprised the whole audience. I added that I came to show, who the true ministers of the Gosple were.

We agreed with the committee consisting of three public speakers, that they should make use of the first opportunity to proclaim the resolutions which have been unanimously adopted in our Convention. Soon after my tremendous "no" one of our committee arose and told the assembled thousands, that a committee sent from an anti-slavery Convention had arrived with most important resolutions, to be publicly read in the grand tent meeting. The chairman replied, that next after the address of the man who occupied the floor, they should deliver their resolutions. They went directly on the platform. But the pharisees on the platform were anxious to find out, who the man was, that gave the strong negative vote to their resolution. Some amongst them knew me personally. Therefore as soon as our committee came upon the platform, the above mentioned Quaker preacher Joseph Dugdale came to me inquiring, whether that committee belonged to my association or not. I said, that he should not ask me, but the committee, to which association they belonged.

One of the deepest English investigators into the Jewish and Christian antiquities wrote in one of his publications, that there is no society more like the society of the Old Pharisees, than the Society of Quakers is. He knew them in England, and I know them in America, and confess that it is true in regard to the Quaker speculators, who have enslaved the whole Quaker society, to be in their servitude and to prepare in their ignorance of matters the subjugation of the whole country under the yoke of monarchs. Joseph Dugdale is the principal medium who was carried soon after that spectacle to Pennsylvania, and demons were powerfully operating through him in starting the sect of the "Progressive Friends." But at that tent meeting he inspired the heads to be cautious in admitting our committee to speak. Therefore after the address of the man after whom our committee according to the promise of the chairman were to address the tent meeting, another was announced by name, to speak, and then a second, a third, and so on, although our committee were waiting on the platform from 9 o'clock A. M. till 2 or 3

P. M. At length the chairman announced, that teams had arrived, to carry the tent from that to another place. Provisions had been made, that if there should be danger for the infernal league, things might be prepared, to break of the tent. Therefore when the chairman announced the advent of the teams, another pharisee mentioned, that the waiting committee had not yet spoken and the chairman said, that they should speak.

The speaker, instead of reading directly the resolutions of our Convention, undertook to prepare the audience by telling them, that he knew how to value the great zeal of Mr. Garrison for the deliverance of slaves. And as far Mr. Garrison and others on the platform seemed to be pleased. But as soon as he mentioned, that "Garrison is not infallible," those who were ready for action, commenced to break off the tent, and there arose such a tumult amongst the assembled people, that nobody could distinguish the voice of the speaker from the noise of the crowd.

These items may suffice, to make known the infallible Pope, the Garrisonian Liberator, although I could write many volumes of extraordinary spirit manifestations in public and private meetings with members of that party, while I was endeavoring to deliver them from the shackles of the infernal Holiness and his armies. But they remained so fastened, as in their "Philanthropic Convention" in Utica, which I attended because we had been informed, that the Poughkeepsie seer, Andrew Jackson Davis, was the principal author of said Convention, or, the principal medium of speculators calculating to extend the government of the infernal liberator by using said Convention. Andrew Jackson Davis is the prince of mediums of spirits, who appear as angels of light, but when they are tried by us, they are made manifest as dreadful deluding and destroying demons. After they had been made manifest to me by his deceiving publications, I tried several times to reach him personally, and to show him his dreadful situation and how he could arrive on our ground. But his cunning demons carried him away from my presence. At length I met with him on the tenth of this month September, 1858, in the "Philanthropic Convention" of Utica. Ira Hitchcock was appointed chairman. His first name means in Latin "wrath" or "vengence," and the second name is in the English language appropriate to the important office which our duped and deceived friend did receive in said Convention. Mr. Davis offered some rules, to be observed in the Convention They were adopted. One of those rules was, that no speaker should occupy more than twenty minutes, except the audience should desire, that after the expiration of twenty minutes he should continue to speak.

Mr. Davis was called, to open the Convention with his speech. It was read from a manuscript and contained a very imposing and deceiving view of the past and the present in the history of mankind. Since his reading lasted more than one hour, I asked after its close, that it should be decided, whether those who open the meeting, should be bound by the adopted rule of twenty minutes, or be permitted to speak or read as long as they would be pleased also when they misrepresent the history in such an absurd manner as the speaker did. No regard was taken of what I said, and they proceeded in singing and speaking.

The afternoon session was opened with as long a reading as the forenoon session. After the reading they debated, whether it should be directly printed in a newspaper of the place and in extra copies, or not. It was unanimously decided that it should be printed, except that I disturbed the unanimous vote with a powerful "no." But when I desired to give my reasons, that its publication would not serve " to overcome evil with good," but to increase the evil, I was stopped, as being not in order in opposition to a resolution which had been unanimously carried out.

For a better understanding of the spectacles which will be mentioned afterwards, we must remark the following incident, which happened on that day, to wit, somebody mentioned, that there came many female mediums from a great distance in the expectation to be moved in the Convention by spirits to speak, that therefore all these mediums should come on the platform, and speak, whenever any of them should be moved by a spirit to do so. I think that others felt the absurdity of that proposition, which if it had been accepted, would have created great confusion and hindrance to the realization of their speculations; therefore they did not respond to his suggestion. Readers should know, that if not all, certainly most of the heads and the agents of that Convention were spiritualists of the latest fashion.

On the afternoon of that day, after singing, I suddenly took the stand, to make use of the twenty minutes time, conceded by the rule of the Convention to every speaker. I wished to show, that nobody in the Convention touched the root of the evil; and that when others have neglected to study our message of Peace, which shows that root and how to extirpate it, at length spiritualists have been urged to do so. But they, instead of progressing and learning by our message, how to overcome evil with good, were attached to evil spirits, and they deluded people regarding our message of Peace, when we endeavored to move them to study it and act accordingly. Instead of many instances of our experience testifying this, I would mention only my experience at the last public meeting of spiritualists which I attended in the City of New York. A female medium whose lying spirits were exposed by me in a public meeting of spiritualists in Philadelphia on the first day of the last month (August 1858) came on the 22d of the same month to a meeting of spiritualists in New-York, in which meeting I spoke. During my speech the demon by whom she was possessed, propelled her three times to stop my speech. But when he was rebuked so terribly, that her friends could not bear any longer, they awakened her from her sleep and carried her out of the hall. But as soon as I ceased to speak, she returned; and the demon shut instantly her eyes, and said through her, that I am a Judas Jscariot, a Jesuit, an emissary of the Pope, &c. The chairman was induced to ask the name of the spirit; but he refused to tell his name. Then he said through his medium, that he is "Donquixote Thomas Paine." The first name he pronounced so that I knew by the pronunciation, who amongst my departed friends was the controller of the lying spirit, by whom the medium was possessed. My departed friend compelled him in the first place to tell, that he was Don Quixote, known as the hero in the celebrated Spanish romance or fable called Don Quixote. A similar fiction was also the speech of the demon by whom that medium was possessed, only that those who do not know me, might take the calumny of the devil for truth. After the confession that he was Don Quixote, to make which he was compelled by a higher power, he added according to his lying propensity, that he was Thomas Paine, although he was not Thomas Paine.

When I desired to explain, from which sphere of spirits that liar came, I was stopped by a man crying behind me to the chairman, asking him whether I should be permitted or not to occupy an hour, while nobody could understand me. At such interruptions I strike sometimes the impudent demons, as they deserve to be stricken. I think, that I did not speak ten minutes, when that interruption took place. To draw my attention from the disturbing demon, Henry C. Wright jumped to me, saying that I should not speak, because I am not understood, and he told the audience that he knew me to be a good man, but that I could not be understood by Americans. I interrupted him saying with indignation, that he did not know me and that those do not understand me, who have ears and will not hear and eyes and will not see. I felt that the audience were not prepared for further explanations; but the truth is, that while I have been speaking English on more than one thousand places in America, those who have acquired some education and paid attention to my discourses, understood me; but enemies of truth complained, that they could not understand me, or they made disturbance. Not to give to demons any opportunity to enrage their mediums against me at the night session of that day, I would not attend that session.

On the 11th inst. at the first opportunity at the forenoon session I offered the resolutions to be read, for a better understanding of which these remarks are a preparation.

But the chairman remarked, that that was not the proper time for reading my resolutions. Then I kept silence at that session. But during the afternoon session I offered several times my resolutions to be read. But Ira Hitchcock always interfered, pointing to some other, that he was in order to speak, although I did not see, that he arose before me for this purpose.

I found proper not to attend any of the following sessions of said Convention, in which I have offered the means, "to overcome evil with good;" but the infernal league hindered their communication to the people, and when the mediums of the infernal league thought, that they were removing evil and promoting good, they were doing just the contrary. If we have the mission which is proved in many of my volumes and expressed at the end of the resolutions for which we are preparing readers by these remarks, then all those who are hindering the circulation of our message of Peace, are the most dreadful slaveholders and destroyers of human life and property. They keep people in shackles of delusion and ignorance of what they should know, to prevent destruction of many and subjugation of the remnant by cruel tyrants.

I saw the report of the proceedings on the first day of the Convention in two Utica daily papers. I quote from the Utica Morning Herald, September 11th, 1858, the following passage regarding my first interference, as follows: "at the conclusion of Mr. Davis' lengthy harangue, a German arose and said," he hopes that those who opens the meetings, speaks no more as twenty minutes, or not! I have prepared a speech on the root of all evil that will not dake so mooch dime as the friends who have speak!" The devil, that means calumniator, by whom this reporter was so possessed, that he knew neither orthography nor grammar, was not so bad as the devil, by whom the evening Telegraph" was possessed He, in the service of the heads of the Convention, calls me "the member from Germany," also "the teutonic individual," and what he reports, he so reports for the benefit of the infernal league according to the wishes of mediums of lying spirits, that I had to write much, if I would explain the cunning malice, which is comprehended in the misrepresentations and lies in regard to the exertions which I made to move the "Philanthropic Convention" to an investigation of my written documents showing that which is first necessary to overcome evil with good. But here not being room, I quote only the following passage, which the Telegraph has published as my saying: "I knew Don Ke Shott; some call him Don Quixote, but I call him Don Ke Shott. I can tell you all about him."

Mediums of lying and destroying spirits have been brought to that Convention from the Cities of New-York, Boston and many other places of several States. To deliver those slaves from their tyrants, I mentioned, that at my last attendance of a public meeting of spiritualists in New-York a female medium was seized by a terrible devil who declared, that I was "Judas Jscariot, an emissary from the Pope, a Jesuit," although after my having been from A. D. 1819, till 1838 a Roman Catholic Priest, I was working since the year 1838, according to my mission, with great zeal for the abolition of all kinds of Popery. On this account I am abused and persecuted not only by the agents of the grand Pope of Rome, but also by such small Popes, as have been assembled in said Philanthropic Convention" as well as by their reporters. I mentioned in my address, that the lying spirit who said through the female medium, that I am a Judas Jscariot, a Jesuit, an emissary from the Pope," did confess then, that he is "Don Quixote Thomas Paine." But that my remark was then so terribly abused, as the above quoted passage testifies. Lying spirits are supported by speakers and by editors of newspapers.

The reader should recollect what I said above regarding Henry C. Wright's assisting his colleague interrupting my speech. The Herald reports it, as follows: "Mr. Wright finally said he had known Smollnikar for some time, he was a very worthy man, but the Convention could not understand him when he tried to speak English." Smollnikar—They have ears and will not hear, they have eyes and will not see."

The Herald has given here the substance and also the name of Mr. Wright. But this did not agree with the position of the heads of the Convention, who have promised free speech, and then one of the principal heads of Abolitionists came as Judas Jscariot to me, and assisted the murderer of my message, with a hypocritical address to the audience, as if he was my best friend. Therefore instead of his name Henry C. Wright there appeared in the Telegraph "a lagerbeer," as if I had spoken so in the Convention, that intoxicated Germans themselves had found it necessary to stop me in my speech.

I did not see any German in the Convention; but it would be too mild to call Henry C. Wright a "lagerbeer." He is a "Wright" or a workman, an emissary of the infernal "Ira Hitchcock," The Latin word "Ira" means the wrath or vengence, which appeared in the chairman Ira Hitchcock, or hitch, that means catch the cock, that he might not cry and awaken people from their lethargy, to save the country from the infernal wrath and vengeance, which is kindled by such emissaries of His Infernal Holiness, as Henry C. Wright is, a blasphemer of the Living God and His Christ, and a rebel against Divine Decrees made manifest in our mission, but which have been despised by Henry C. Wright, Ira Hitchcock and other heads of said Convention. Those rebels against God and His Christ had many years ago opportunity to learn the Divine Decrees for redemption of oppressed humanity; but they have conspired also in their last Convention, to check their proclamation and to open the infernal crater of a volcano to destroy the country by rebellion and other crimes, which have been openly defended by Henry C. Wright and others in that Convention, in which by our mission the means were offered to abolish all kinds of slavery in a peaceable manner.

In my signature at the end of the resolutions as well as in my publications, you find my name correctly written. But the mentioned reporters were mediums of deluding and destroying spirits by whom they were magnetized and were made deaf and blind, so that they thought, I was a German; although they should have so much sense of discernment, and judgment, as to know from my pronunciation, that I am not a German. If I had been a German, I could not have received the mission with which I am charged—because the messenger in the mission with which I am charged, must come, according to prophecies, from the Slavonian nation, from the country called Illyria or Illyricum, from the town, named in my mother tongue Kamnik, in Greek and Latin Lithopolis, in German Stein, in English Stone.

Against the impudence with which also my language was so terribly misrepresented there is no room to make more than this remark :

A. D. 1835, I wrote a Latin treatise " On the congeniality of languages," showing how by the comparative study of languages many deep truths for the introduction of Christ's peaceable Reign or of the universal Republic of Truth and Justice would be unravelled. Before I was qualified to write such a treatise, I had to study many ancient and modern languages, some more thoroughly, and some only by looking over the grammar and dictionary. Here is no room to explain the reasons, why I devoted, before writing said treatise, only some few hours and learned more than the Herald and the Telegraph and other scoffers of our mission have learned all their life time regarding the etymology of their own English mother tongue. If they cannot comprehend this our assertion without our explanation, I am ready to explain it in an article, if they promise to publish it in their newspapers : because it may awaken many scholars for co-operation with us to introduce the new Era of Union and Peace of nations, who have in their ignorance of matters worked until now for disunion of nations and for destruction of human life and property.

We hope, that editors and publishers of newspapers, who have by their reports misrepresented our mission, will not remain mediums of lying and destroying spirits, but will, as their duty requires, publish this article, and comprehend the importance of the preceding remarks as well as of the " Resolutions " which follow and what is annexed to the resolutions, to move the American nation and by their mediumship all nations for action, to redeem oppressed humanity from the yoke of tyrants, and that those for whom it would be impossible, to publish the whole in one number, will publish it in two or three numbers. Our resolutions have been offered to the Convention in the following words ;

Resolutions for the "Philanthropic Convention to overcome evil with good," held in Utica on the 10th, 11th, and 12th September 1858.

Whereas the writer of the following resolutions did hear nothing in this Convention of "the general fundamental cause of the existing evils in the social, religious and political relations of mankind," and according to his knowledge in no Convention of the so called reformers has this general fundamental cause been found out, and will not be comprehended by them, till they come on the ground which the writer occupies, according to his mission, which is made manifest in the documents which have been offered to be read in this Convention. When those documents will be read and comprehended, the following resolutions will be adopted:

Resolved 1st, that the general fundamental cause of the evils which are to be removed from the social, political and religious relations of mankind, is founded in the Old Heavens and in the Old Earth, that means the old institutions, which will be removed when they shall be comprehended by true reformers, since the so called reformers who are warring against those institutions from their materialistic position, are supporting those institutions, because they are mediums of those spirits who are subject to and controlled by the Papal Imperial Royal Spirits, so that materialism and the modern spiritualism are the last outbreaks of Popery, and materialists and modern spiritualists are the means of the outbreak of the worst evils, which remain latent, till the materialistic spirits come in collision with the rules given by their controllers, the Popish spirits. From this collision of spirits originate riots, wars and other evils, which will be removed, when the pretended reformers and mediums of deluding and destroying spirits will receive the light which has been kindled by the mediumship of the writer.

Resolved 2d, That the particular and in the exterior life of people manifest evils, which are easily observed by those materialists who are falsely called reformers, cannot be removed from the society, till true reformers understand the real position of the existing churches and the spiritualism in the churches as well as the modern spiritualism out of the churches; because without this understanding there is neither knowledge nor strength in the so called reformers, to effect the true reformation, and to establish the promised Peace amongst all nations, for which the means are developed in the publications and manuscripts of the writer of these resolutions.

It is expected, that those who have called this Convention, and those who attend it are not so blind that they having called a Convention to overcome evil with good," and granted freedom of speech in this Convention, this freedom being accepted by the assembly, would reject the good which is offered by the writer to overcome evil; since the writer affirms that those who are anxious to speak in this Convention, have nothing to say, which has not been already many times repeated in Conventions, if it is for any use at all to remove evil, but that the writer has to communicate matters to remove evil, which are not known to those who attend this Convention, as will be evident, if the two documents which are offered to be read in this Convention, and which have been written, one the last month, and the other during the travelling of the writer from New-York to this Convention, will be read publicly to this assembly. The writer remarks especially in regard to the mediums of spirits by whom they have been brought, to speak with closed eyes in this Convention, that from the documents offered to be read, it will be made manifest, that their spirits are deluding spirits, from whom the mediums will be delivered, and enlightened by spirits of Truth, if they study with attention the writings which have been produced by the mediumship of the writer who signs his name and the charges which he has received for the introduction of the New Heaven.

ANDREW B. SMOLNIKER, &c. see title page.

Neither this lengthy nor other shorter articles which have been offered since that time to editors of newspepers did suit their taste in the general corruption of the press. I saw since that time, to wit in December, 1858, again personally Mr. Garrisson in his office in Boston, but he was as stubborn in his pernicious course as in former times. I called very seldom, when I was in Philadelphia, in the "Garrisonian" antislavery office. But it happened, I think, towards the end of the winter season, A. D. 1858, while I was passing that office, that I was impressed to enter it. I found there a rich Mulatto with whom I had been acquainted for years, but who was so chained by the Garrisonian imposition, that although I walked several times some miles from Philadelphia to teach him in his house, how our master had decreed to deliver slaves by co-operation of slaveholders themselves, the rich Mulatto had never time to study our message of Peace, although he seemed to burn with great zeal for redeeming slaves, and he and his wife had superabundance of time to attend antislavery meetings and conventions and to perform all prescriptions of "the Garrisonian Liberator." At that my meeting with him in the "Antislavery Office" I understood from his conversation with others, that they had appointed a meeting at candle-light of that day, and that that Mulatto was by virtue of his office president of that meeting. I did not inquire, for what antislavery purpose that meeting was appointed, and without asking this I said to the Mulatto, that I was also inclined to attend that meeting, if he would tell after their meeting to the audience, that I had a message which would need no more than three minutes time, and that my message would not interfere with their meeting. The rich Mulatto accepted my offer.

That meeting was held in a large church of the colored people and the church was crowded. But I was quite surprised, when I understood from their proceedings and harangues, that it was an "underground railroad" meeting, in which they disclosed so much of their secret proceedings of the transportation of slaves to Canada, and endeavored by their revolutionary speeches to kindle the animal passions of the audience to rebellion that if such a meeting would have been held in France or Austria or several other monarchies, all speakers would have been imprisoned in the State's Prison and if not all, certainly several of them would have remained perpetually in prison. After their meeting the rich Mulatto chairman announced, that I had to deliver a short message independent from their meeting. I mentioned briefly, that I am a messenger of Peace, having superabundance of credentials for delivering slaves by co-operation of slaveholders themselves, if abolitionists would learn our message and give good example to slaveholders; and that, since there was no time for an explanation of the matter, they should appoint a committee to whom a manuscript of mine should be read, containing that which those should know, who are working for redemption of slaves. A committee of five colored men was appointed; but at our first meeting all members of the committee were not present, and those who came to the first meeting were so distracted with other business, that they did not pay attention to what has been read the first time, and the others had their excuses to come again, except a Mulatto from West India who would have persevered, if others had done the same. But he alone could do nothing, because he was not a long time in Philadelphia and had not much influence there.

I have given here one case of my experience, instead of hundreds of cases, how dreadfully the colored people are duped and deceived by the heads of antislavery armies, while these heads or popes appear to have great zeal for deliverance of slaves, although they are the cause, that some of them are killed, and those who are brought to Canada, become more miserable slaves than they have been before, because they are drilled in weapons to kill and be killed, while our master offers by our instrumentality to the anti-slavery champions the means to deliver white and black slaves from all forms of oppresion and slavery. But there are many, under the specious name of the antislavery cause, agents of monarchs and traitors of the true Republican or true anti-slavery cause. And those who are not directly bribed by monarchial agents for the conversion of this country into monarchies, are mediums or instruments of deluding and destroying spirits, by whom they are so blinded that they really believe, that they are working "for deliverance of the poor slave," while they are assisting monarchs, to enslave the whole country.

I think that our friend Gerrit Smith is such a medium. We have tried to convert him many years ago from his delusion, and after previous preparations which we have made in his house, it was, I think, on the 18th of February, 1845, (which is the anniversary of great events in our mission,) that I met with him in a convention of antislavery ministers and other abolitionists, which was held in Syracuse, N. Y. He was chairman. A number of resolutions for operations in the antislavery movements had been read and adopted. Then I arose and assured the audience, that if my document which I had prepared for that occasion, would be read, they could comprehend that those resolutions would be for no use, and that better means have been providentially prepared for the redemption of slaves by co-operation of slaveholders themselves, if anti-slavery champions would study to know those means and make use of them. The chairman Gerrit Smith asked the audience, whether my document should be read. The majority answered " Yes." He asked the votes of those who would be against its reading. Some voices were heard, that it should not be read. And the chairman Smith said : " Smolnikar, you have lost the floor. He was right, if the Convention was ruled by those who had made the resolutions and by their colleagues. And I said, that if they would not receive light, they should continue in darkness, and I left directly. At length rapping spirits broke out and had great influence in his house, because he shut his eyes, when light has been offered to him from the spirit of truth by our mediumships. I tried in different times to move our friend Gerrit Smith to study our message and the credentials of our mission. But deluding and destroying spirits drew him in other directions. At length A. D. 1854 I tried particularly to move the Congress of the United States to appoint a Convention in which I promised to exhibit the means to deliver this country from monarchial influence and to establish the promised universal Republic of Truth, Justice and Peace on earth, and the credentials of our mission, and I applied to a number of congressmen in both Houses to bring the subject before their respective bodies. At length, when all others had neglected to fulfil this their highest duty, I applied to Hon. Gerrit Smith, who was at that time in the House of Representatives

I mention strange things ; but they will not appear strange, if readers keep in mind, that I represent the body of messengers, who are collectively called the third angel in REVEL. xiv: 9. In this book I give on many subjects only hints; otherwise I should have to write also a large volume of wonders and signs which happened, while I was trying in that year President Pierce and members of the cabinet and the congress. But if editors of the Tribune wish besides what I offered in the first treatise to show regarding their pet Fremont, that they might commence to be sober in forwarding candidates for high offices, I would like to write also an other article comparing Hon. Gerrit Smith with Senator Seward and to publish what happened while I was trying both in Washington City; because at that our trial it was in an extraordinary manner made manifest, that although Gerrit Smith was badly chained by the spirit of delusion, Senator Seward was found much more chained than Genit Smith. On this account our leaders moved me at the last campaign of candidates for governor of the State of New York, A. D.1858, and I was acting in my mission in that State, while Gerrit Smith was proclaimed candidate by his party so that I wrote to him, what he had to do, to be favored by our leaders in his course for a high office; because the time has at length arrived in which our leaders will commence to show publicly, how they have the power to interfere in the election business of officers. And then candidates for offices and officers will commence to see the necessity of studying our message and the credentials for our mission, to become with us messengers of Peace, and people will commence to abhor electing such as are so degraded, that they are not prepared to study the Heavenly message made manifest for the redemption of oppressed humanity and the establishment of the promised universal Republic. But how until now those who have been solemnly warned by us, to do what they as professing to be Republicans and occupying high offices, were particularly bound to do, have neglected to fulfil their highest duty, we will show with few instances, that those who will be named, might arise from death to life, and all readers might be inspired for co-operation with us, since Providence is instructing mankind by so remarkable cases, as are the following:

At the commencement of the year 1856 I arrived in Columbus, Ohio, and endeavored to move the Republican anti-slavery Governor Chase and the Republican Party which was the strongest in the legislature of Ohio, to co-operation with us to establish the universal Republic of Peace on earth. For this purpose I wrote "an address to the legislature and the citizens of Ohio" and sent the manuscript with an urgent recommendation to Governor Chase, that he after having perused the manuscript might forward it with his recommendation to the legislature of Ohio. In my manuscript or my written address to the legislature as many testimonies of our mission were mentioned as would have been sufficient to move a man who has discernment in spiritual things, for co-operation with us, But the Governor, after having perused my manuscript in which I urged the legislature by virtue of the memorable events which have been mentioned in it, to appoint a monthly theological course, to which qualified persons would be invited to hear the explanation of my manuscript which contains the system for the foundation of the universal Republic, and for the commencement of the New Era called the millennium, said when he returned it to me, that he was not the proper person to forward the manuscript to the legislature. I do not know, whether he would have entered into a discussion of the matter, if I had offered him to show, that he was not only the proper person, but that it was his most urgent duty to forward my address to the legislature. I thought that he in his new highest office of that State was too much distracted and was not prepared for our extraordinary business. Wherefore I sent that same address which was directed to the legislature of Ohio, to the speaker in the House, and instructed him in an extra letter of his duty, to forward my address to the House. But he belonged to the Republican Party and had no capacity for what was needed to establish the true Republic of Harmony and Peace on earth, and could not be moved to do, what was shown to him to be most necessary in his circumstances. He returned my address. From him I went to the Lieutenant Governor or speaker in the Senate. He belonged to the American Party and by his application the Senate appointed a committee for examining my document. In that committee was a member of the Republican Party, who assured his colleagues, that he knew me, that I was a madman, having come from Geauga County in which I held a Convention in the year 1851. Notwithstanding the most malicious conspiracy of the Sectarian neighborhood we succeeded so far, that a number of resolutions in which I have concentrated what has been explained in the Convention for the commencement of the millennium, have been unanimously adopted, and then published with other documents for an easier understanding of the resolutions. But materialists, papists and other sectarians, instead of having reflected upon the unexpected glorious news made manifest in that pamphlet and put them into circulation, did all in their power that the largest portion of copies of that pamphlet and the man to whom they have been given in care, disappeared, and the calumny was put into circulation, that I became mad. And when that same calumny was renewed in the Senate chamber of Ohio, I wrote a resolution, to be offered to that body. But members of the Senate became so scared, that I could find nobody, to undertake to offer it to the Senate. I wished by that resolution to move the Senate to give me their chamber for a lecture, in which I wished to explain the madness of those who instead of studying our disclosures for Harmony and Peace of nations, are slandering and calumniating me, and ruining this country and preparing it more and more to become a spoil to enrich monarchs and their agents.

Then I published that address and other documents which I supposed, would be strong enough to move the legislature and other citizens of Ohio to send qualified persons to the monthly theological course, which was appointed in that pamphlet.

Here we must extract passages from the last page for a great lesson to Republicans and others that they might not be duped any longer by the blind leaders of the blind. That page contains "a great appeal to the Governor, the Senate and House of Representatives of the State of Ohio." It was written, mark well, on the 2d day of February, as is mentioned on that 32d page as well, as on the pages 31 and 29; because on the 29th page I commenced to write a paragraph as follows: "I had to wait till the composition of this epistle advanced so far, that I must finish it on this 2d day of February" &c. On that day I wrote what follows from that passage to the end of the pamphlet. And the "great appeal" reads: "Fellow laborers in the great cause of human redemption! If you have studied this pamphlet with such attention as it deserves to be studied you will accept this title with gratitude to the Most High, that he has chosen us in his mercy for the accomplishment of the most glorious promises" . . "The first most urgent work" (which the legislature of Ohio in those circumstances could do) "is to kindle with this pamphlet a light in the Cabinet and the Congress of the United States. "And Babylon is become a habitation of demons." REVEL. xviii: 2. The fall of Babylon has been proclaimed by my instrumentality for the fulfilment of the first three verses of the 18th chapter of the REVELATION, on Easter Sunday, 1838, under the direction of the powerful angel, who was sent from the Heavenly Congress. And since that proclamation, the habitation of demons on every place of Babylon, on which my message is rejected, is made manifest . . and the numbers of votes which members of the House of Representatives were casting since my first publication of the "testimony for the superabundance of miracles," which is reprinted on the 9th and 10th pages of this pamphlet, are testifying, from which quarters of pitfalls and deep holes the demons came who took possession of the Capitol at the present session. . . . On this 2nd day of February in my Country Roman Catholic men and women bring each his own candle into the church and burn them" &c.

I quoted these passages, written on the 2d day of Feb., which was Saturday, and given on the same day to the printer; because I had an engagement on the next following day in the country and left Columbus on that Saturday, Feb, 2d 1856. When I returned on the next following week from the country, I heard that on that same day February 2d, 1856, the House of Representatives finished at length their voting for speaker and that Nathanael Banks was elected Speaker in the House. There is a spirit language by numbers. Representatives in the House were casting votes from the time in which my article "Testimony for the superabundance of miracles" appeared in two newspapers of Cleveland and was then copied in my pamphlet for the legislature of Ohio, to make use of it for the conversion of the Congress in Washington; because I saw, whenever I looked the numbers of votes cast to elect the speaker, that members of the parties casting votes were under a strong Papal Imperial Royal delusion. When I wrote the above quoted passages on the 2nd day of February, 1856, I did not know, that at that same time they finished their voting with Nathanael Banks as speaker in the House. Nathanael means a "gift of God." And the name Banks was prophetical for what followed then in regard to the Banks; because this generation could receive no more suitable gift than Banks are. There is not only in numbers but also in names and in manifold other correspondences a spirit language which we understand; and in this our mission events connected with our steps testify the condition in which those are, who neglect to make use of our message of Peace. The Governor and the legislature of Ohio did not care about our urgent appeal made to them in writing and in print, and the same time in Washington the name of Banks announced the terrible condition of this same country founding their trust in banks and paper-money, which will be eventually made manifest with a terrible crash.

After that experience made at the Republican Legislature of Ohio, in which we could not find assistance for the circulation of our message of Peace, and for holding our monthly theological course, I remained in Ohio, till I heard Governor Chase in a campaign for candidate Fremont assert with great boldness, that he knew Fremont. I did not know Fremont at that time. But after having studied as much as was required to know him, I pitied Governor Chase and other Republicans very much, that they either by ignorance of matters or by preferring private interest to the common welfare, should have ruined the country and destroyed an enormous amount of human life and property, so that the Kansas affairs alone cost more than fifty millions of dollars. All the evils would have been avoided, if Hon. Giddings and his co-operators who have been most urgently invited to attend the above mentioned Convention which was held in their vicinity in the year 1851, had not despised our invitation. But at that time matters had not arrived to that maturity in which they are now. And we write and mention some champions and leaders of parties, that they themselves and by their instrumentality many others might be awakened from their lethargy and attend at length our monthly theological course the appointment of which they will find at the end of this book, and learn that which is most needed for the support of the true Republican, or what is the same, true christian against the monarchial cause.

I have sent to speaker Banks a copy of the pamphlet, from the last page of which I have quoted above some passages, on which page there is the admirable correspondence of the governor and the legislature of Ohio with his election for speaker. But I think, that other trifling business did hinder Mr. Banks' comprehending wonders and signs contained in that pamphlet, and that he did not study it so deep as to comprehend the correspondence of the contents of the last page of said pamphlet with his election for speaker on the same day on which I wrote that page. In this book is no room to explain the language by numbers; but we may generally observe, that the election took place under the spell of the Papel Imperial Royal spirits; and it was said, that it did not happen, till a Roman catholic priest came into the House of Representatives and performed his prayer. Whether that report was true or not, it is not my business to investigate; but it is true, that the spell was taken away, when I in my application to the governor and the legislature of Ohio wrote on the last page of the above quoted pamphlet: " You are requested to cast so many copies of this pamphlet in the Cabinet and Congress of Washington, and also into the legislature of each State, as are required to kindle a great light everywhere." Reference is made to the " Candle-mass," as the feast of the 2d February is called. It is Mary's purification and Christ's presentation in the temple; and that our reference to the casting of votes for the speaker in the House of the United States destroyed the spell and they agreed at length in the prophetical name Banks, with which there was already great trouble, and the greater troubles will follow, the longer nations delay to apply our remedies against the manifold enormous evils with which nations are harrassed and ruined. I made some acquaintance with Governor Banks after my last arrival in Boston in Nov.1858. I found proper to write to him a lengthy letter in which I assured him, that if he would become a great supporter of the true Republican cause, he would nead some private lessons to know what happened in our age for the introduction of the universal Republic of Harmony and Peace; because without that knowledge he in the present course of the Republican Party would contribute his share not for Peace, but for revolutions and war. I offered in that letter to give him some private lessons in his house, if he would wish to receive them regarding our message of Peace and the credentials of our mission, and I added, that in that season of short days and long nights there would be at candle-light good opportunity for our lessons. I went then to his house in Waltham, several miles from Boston. But on that evening he had not yet returned from his office, and I was informed, that on the next morning would be the best chance to speak with him. I then went there but he had not much time to speak, because he had to go to his office, and he invited me to see him in his office. From that circumstance I concluded, that he did not keep in mind the contents of my letter in which I assured him, that his office would not be the proper place for our lessons, but that the night hours in his house would suit best for our lessons; but then there was no time to expostulate with him on this point. I started then for New Hampshire, and at my return to Boston I wrote to him again, that I intended to see him again, but not in his office which would not be the proper place for our lessons, but in his house, that if he would be desirous to receive lessons, I would remain for some days in his village and give to him lessons at candle-light. I came then to his village, and prepared one of his acquaintances, a zealous spiritualist, who appeared to comprehend easier than other spiritualists, that Presidents, Governors and other officers cannot save this Republic from the grasp of monarchs except by the use of the spiritual weapons which are concentrated in my writings for the commencement of the promised New Era, and that Governor Banks to use his influence for Harmony and Peace of all nations, had to take lessons from me. When I thought, that the spiritualist partly by hearing me partly by reading one of my pamphlets had understood the matter so far as necessary to move the Governor to accept my proposition, he went to see Governor Banks. But he returned with the message, that the Governor had started for Hartford.

I could not stay longer in Waltham and understood from this circumstance that Governor Banks was not the officer, who would commence to open the door at the government for commencing the the New Era. I thought that if he would comprehend our message, by his instrumentality the Legislature of Massachusetts and by their instrumentality the Congress of the United States might be moved for using our spiritual weapons against the anti-Republican powers. I heard in November 1858, in the night before the election of the Governor and the congress members Governor Banks deliver his speech in Chelsea City. He affirmed that he did not speak for himself but for his friend Burlingame, that he might be re-elected for Congress. I heard this same Burlingame haranguing against Buchanan and for Fremont during the last Presidential campaign, and understood that his speech was nothing else but a heap of "burly games." Mark well, that in our meetings with remarkable persons, names are expressive, but sometimes their signification is so hidden, that some letter is to be changed, to be understood. The great heap of burly games spread in newspapers and in public speeches against Buchanan instead of studying our message of Peace and communicating it to President Buchanan to save the country, prove nothing else except that this degraded generation are preparing the way to such a tyranny as will destroy the largest part and chain the remnant of the people in such a manner that no word will be heard against the cruelty and tyranny which will keep them in slavery, if they do not sooner open their eyes and make use of our message of Peace. I thougt, that if Governor Banks would be converted, he would convert also his friend Burlingame and act through him in the congress. I came after that in Boston, to the office of Governor Banks to see him there; but I was told, that he was expected to be in half an hour in the office. But instead of waiting at, or returning to the office, I was told by my leader, that I had accomplished my mission in the State of Massachussetts and was carried directly to other States.

Wonders and signs which have been given in Boston and Chelsea City near Boston at that my visit there, are spoken of in the following treatise. But before we finish this treatise, we should mention somewhat regarding the Governor of New York in connexion with the Governors of Ohio and Massachussetts. We do not take any interest in the campaign for officers, except when we are directed by our leaders to give in this way a great lesson to nations: as it was the case in the first treatise of this book.

While I intended in Summer, 1858, to start from Philadelphia for the West, I was directed by my leaders to New-York. I arrived the same hour in the City of New-York, in which the laying of the Atlantic Cable had been accomplished, and while spiritualists were rejoicing in a public meeting at the success, in the supposition that the success was certain and that it was a great blessing for the United States, I explained in that meeting, that the success would be a great scourge for this country, if people would not receive our message of Peace and convert monarchs into true Republicans. My explanation was then confirmed by signs. After the exchange of President Buchanan's message with the message of Queen Victoria the use of the Atlantic Telegraph has been suspended by invisible agency, and while the City of New-York, the great Babylon of the United States, was celebrating the first time the success of the Atlantic Telegraph, the tower, the cupola and so much of the interior of the building of the City Hall was destroyed, as could be reached by fire. And at the second solemn celebration of the success of the Atlantic Telegraph the whole Quarantine with numerous buildings was destroyed by fire. The materialistic spectators who looked only on the surface, were not aware of the interior agency. But in connexion with these warning fires other signs were given testifying also in this connexsion of matters the subjugation of this country by Papal Imperial Royal or Monarchial spirits, while citizens of the United States are not yet aware of.

I wrote a peculiar treatise on those signs, which will be published in due time. There was a coalescence of strange correspondences, While the Queen of England was celebrating with Emperor Napoleon the tremendous naval exhibition at Cobourgh, for the subjugation of the world by monarchs, the laying of the Atlantic Telegraph was accomplished and the President of the United States exchanged the message with the Queen; and the destroying fires accompanied the celebration of its success, till at length also the Crystal Palace was consumed by fire; and the spirits who are subject to Popish prelates and monks, announced the "Philanthropic Convention in Utica," and the Archbishop of New-York laid the corner stone to his new cathedral by the assistance of six suffragan bishops. All these in connexion with other memorable events happened according to the spirit language of the prophetical calendar, and I was directed to perform corresponding memorable actions which are explained in this treatise, and amongst those actions here I mention the trial of the three candidates for the Governor's office of the State of New-York. I have already remarked, that I wrote to Hon. Gerrit Smith after he had been proclaimed candidate by his party. But when he was not ready to become messenger of the New Era, I wrote then two lengthy articles, one to be used by Judge Parker, the Democratic candidate, if he would receive our message, and another to be used by the merchant Morgan, the candidate of the Republican Party. I do not belong to any party, and I had only to try spirits of the candidates for Governor in the State in which is the concentration of all monarchial speculations, against which and for the true Republican cause only that Governor could act with power, who would have so much understanding in spiritual things as to comprehend the substance of our message and of the credentials of our mission. Such a man would be a blessing not only for his State, but for the whole country. Both my articles have been written in a manner, that only that Candidate could make use of the article prepared for his use, who would be convinced of our mission, which I intended to explain to him privately, if he would take an interest in my article.

Here follows only a synopsis of our trials of spirits at the two candidates, to wit, the Democratic and the Republican for the office of Governor in the State of New York.

According to the direction of our leaders I paid first my personal visit to Judge Parker of Albany, Democratic Candidate. He appointed a certain time for an interview in which he would be ready to read my writing and hear what I had to say. But when I would return at the appointed time, my leader interfered and said, that I had to try the spirits of merchant Morgan of the City of New York, Candidate of the Republican Party. Morgan appeared to be shrewd as I supposed him to be; because otherwise, having commenced in poverty he would not have become a rich merchant. When I mentioned my business with him, he replied that he had a business, which he must attend in the city, and that his clerk who was in that room, would settle my business with him; and he left the room. Then I talked with his young clerk and mentioned my former charges and my present charge, as far as he may have been able to bear, and that I had with me a document which I had prepared for that campaign. I added, that whereas I belong to no party, that candidate would be most qualified for the Governor's office, who would comprehend my document and make use of it. The clerk insisted, that I should go with my document to the editors of the Tribune. But I replied, that my document was not prepared for the Tribune, but to be studied and used by the candidate himself. But the clerk remarked, that Mr. Morgan would not have time to study it. And I said, that if Mr. Morgan would not have time, I would go to Judge Parker; and I assured the Clerk, that if Judge Parker would have time to study my document and to make use of it, he would certainly become Governor. Then the clerk was moved, that he appointed the hour of the next following day, in which I could speak with Mr. Morgan. I came at the appointed hour; but Mr. Morgan spoke with another man, and when he saw me, he went with his man in an other room. In the mean time the clerk insisted, that I should go with my document to the editors of the Tribune. I did not leave directly the room but was waiting till Mr. Morgan dispatched his man. Then without speaking with me a word he went to other business.

After that my experience I thought that in our dealings with material men we must be provided with very tangeable arguments. I made shortly before that trial acquaintance with a stubborn materialist in the City of New York. He had great iufluence upon people of certan classes, and had all his trust in weapons of iron to put down monarchs. I found him accessible at the point of human magnetism and convinced him by degrees so far, that he confessed that the weapons of the spirit were the right weapons to overcome the monarchial powers. He was, when I made acquaintance with him, running against Judge Parker. But I came after my trial of Mr. Morgan to him, showing that Judge Parker was amongst the three candidates the man who if he would comprehend our message of Peace, would work powerfully for the true Republican cause, During my explanation he was inspired to do all in his power for Judge Parker's election, if the Judge should settle matters with me and pay the expenses for what was to be published in German and in English circulars from each position separately, to be put in circulation in all directions of the State of New-York. That man gave me then in writing the promise to excercise all his influence for Judge Parker's election, if the Judge settles with me the matter.

It is to be repeated, that I according to my mission, am working not for any pay or reward, but only for the great cause of my mission, satisfied with simple food and raiment, which I get when needed, from those who understand that I am working without pay for the great community of mankind. The man who gave me the above mentioned written promise gave me also money to pay my fare from New-York to Albany. I arrived there on a Sunday morning, which was the best time for trying Judge Parker's spirit. I explained to him briefly the reasons why I could not come at the appointed time, without mentioning the invisible direction; because I supposed that the Judge was not yet prepared to comprehend spiritual things. But I insisted, that he, to secure his election, had to spend that Sunday in studying my writings instead of going to church; for he mentioned that I did not come the proper time to him, because he was preparing to go in the church. I showed to him the title page of my pamphlet; "Redemption of oppressed humanity! Christ's manifestation by his messengers for the Abolition of all kinds of Popery." On that page not only my former offices in Babylon are expressed, but also my present office is mentioned, by virtue of which I represent the messengers by whom the promised New Era will be introduced. If he had read the title page on which the substance of our message is concentrated and our mission is expressed, with such attention as to comprehend it and to reflect upon it, he could have understood, that to spend that Sunday with me was exceedingly more important than to attend his sectarian church. I repeated that to study my documents on that Sunday was most important for him.

Two things seemed to deter him from receiving my advice. In the first place he saw on the title page, that I, after having been eighteen years Roman Catholic Priest, appeared in public for the abolition of all kinds of Popery. He may have been afraid to scare Roman Catholics from voting for him, if he would be in any connexion with me. I found not proper to explain, that what I intended to publish in behalf of his election, would not scare but strengthen Roman Catholics to vote for him, but would scare many Republicans and Abolitionists to vote for their candidates and would draw them to him. In the second place he seemed to have been in the same opinion in which I found Democratic editors of newspapers, who told me expressly that they were certain, that their candidate would be Governor. When I found him not ready to study my document on Sunday instead of going into his sectarian church, I did not show him the writing of the champion who was determined to act under the above mentioned condition for Judge Parker's election, but I reported directly to that champion that which happened at my trial of Judge

Parker's spirits and I started straightways for the States of New England.

Attentive readers of this treatise do comprehend, why in the cloud of witnesses of our mission amongst the men and women of the so called Republican Party I selected the three acting Governors, Hon. Chase of Ohio, Banks of Mass. and Hon. Morgan of New York They appear, because they are Headmen of the three most dangerous States to the true Republican cause. Those are the principal States from which there is spread also into other States much zeal for freedom of nations without knowledge of the means for the true freedom. This their zeal instead of promoting the true Republican cause is promoting the cause of monarchs and ruining this country. I could write much in connexion with these three Governors for a warning example to all Governors and all other officers; but these few hints may suffice, that all might know the necessity to study our message of Peace, to promote in their offices the true Democratic or true Republican cause and establish Peace on the whole globe. There is a general hue raised by Republicans, that there is great corruption at the Federal Government. There is in all parties and sects a general and exceedingly great corruption; and we must repeat, that those political and ecclesiastical heads who belong to the parties of Abolitionists and Republicans, are the principal cause of the horrible degradation and corruption, by which this country is ruined; because since the time in which I commenced to urge the American nation by English addresses and publications, my principal applications were especially to those who profess to belong to the parties of Republicans and Abolitionists. If they had studied our message of Peace and had applied the remedy which is comprehended in it against all kinds of degradation and corruption, we would have seen several years ago the fruits of our work. But when they in their degradation and corruption, instead of having received our message of Peace, did all in their power to stop it, as I have shown, instead of hundreds of instances of our experience only by the remarkable specimen of the Utica Philanthropic Convention, they are to be regarded as the principal cause of such awful warnings, as a specimen was given on Sunday Sexagesima, February 27th 1859, on the President's Square of Washington by the executive power of our leader who has REVEL. xiv : 14 a sickle in his hand, and will make use of "sickles" to sweep away the scoundrels and corruptors of females. Their abominations will come to day-light in this "Judgment Dispensation," when the criminals will least expect. The farther you proceed in reading and understanding this book, the more light you will receive in regard to the inner life of man and to the world of spirits, to know the secret enemies of true Republicanism, and how to stop the degradation and corruption, by which Republic is destroyed and monarchy or tyranny is established.

We have selected in the first treatise such facts as should inspire every reader and especially Democrats for co-operation with us, and the facts made public in this treatise, should move especially the parties of Abolitionists and Republicans. We will see, whether President Buchanan's friends or the heads of his opposition will hear sooner the voice of our master made manifest by our mediumship for Harmony and Peace of all nations, and awaken not only the Government of the United States but also other governments from their lethargy.

Human degradation and corruption having been sheltered under the cloak of virtue, and under the specious name of "Free Love" careless males and female having been ruined in body and soul, peculiar opportunity was given us to close this treatise with a brief report on "a treatise on the second coming of Christ. By John H. Noyes, Putney, Vt. 1840," because that treatise was handed to me on this 19th day of March, while I am travelling through Cumberland County, Pa. and by what happened at the reception of that treatise I was aware, that a brief report would suit best for closing this our treatise. On the 29th page of that treatise we read; "Now Swedenborg preached that the second coming of Christ took place in 1757, and that he was himself an eye witness of the transaction. Ann Lee, the mother of the Shakers, preached that the second coming took place in 1770, and that Christ made his appearance in her person. Many similar proclamations have been made from time to time, along the whole period of Christian history, and especially since the Reformation. The latest of this fashion that has come to our notice, is Professor Andreas Bernardus Smolnikar, who teaches that Christ appeared in 1836, and appointed him "Ambassador Extraordinary" (Mr. Noyes quotes as his authority "Signs of the times," No. 12. p. 95. Then he continues his tale as follows:) "of all these we may say fearlessly, as Paul says, "though they be Angels from Heaven, let them be accursed" they have denied the word of God—together with these, another class of visionaries and impostors, less presumptuous, but equally foolish, may be noticed. We refer to those who either by pretended revelation, or by interpretation, have undertaken, from time to time within the last few centuries, to prophesy of the near approach of the second advent. The latest and most notable specimen of this class, is William Miller, who at this time, is confidently proclaiming, 1843 is the appointed year of the second coming".

I would not have noticed "Noyes's treaties," if it had not been unexpectedly handed to me, when I came, while I thought I was going into the house of a man with whom I was acquainted, to his brother whom I did not know until yesterday, when I came against my expectation to him. He commenced to tell that he had a pamphlet in which Mr. Noyes speaks about me. Then he has shown the above quoted passage in Noyes's pamphlet. But I did not yet think to take notice of it, till at length he has brought this morning the pamphlet to his brother-in-law, with whom I stopped last night, and I found proper to quote the passage and to write this edition for the conclusion of this treatise. But the quoted passage is in such connexions and correspondences, that in a new large treatise I could not explain them. Here we can report only the following items.

In the year 1840, on Easter Saturday, my third German volume of "memorable events" issued from the press. Those three volumes exhibit the "magnetic chain" of events to bind the dragon or serpant, the image of the spirit of delusion and destruction, who inspires snch "extraordinary ambassadors, as John H. Noyse is. That he belongs to those deceivers who have deluded those who belong to the Anti-slavery and Republican Parties, and are opposed to our message of Peace, is evident by the circumstance, that I commenced this treatise with the three angels or ambassadors or messengers of the 14th chapter of the Revel., the 3d amongst whom commences his message in the 9th verse of that chapter. I mentioned that each of those angels or messengers represents a body or society of messengers, and that Dr. Bengel has pointed out in the first part of the last century, that Christ will be made manifest about the year 1836; but that neither Dr. Bengel nor any other man did know the manner in which he was to be made manifest, till it was disclosed by the 3d Angel Revel. xiv: 9, or the representative of angels or ambassadors or messengers by whom the contents of the prophecy xiv. 9, 10, 11, must be fulfilled. Interpreters did not understand many other things nor those verses till they may read their explanation in my above quoted three German volumes. I do not recollect, how I did entitle that my address; but it did not contain 95 pages nor was it published in several numbers, so that I did not know what those "signs of the times" were, to which Noyse has reference, except that Joshuah Himes, the head of the Millerite imposition was publishing at that time a paper, entitled "Signs of the Times," and since he announced, that he would publish also such views regarding Christ's coming, which were not in accordance with the views of his sect, I expected to open the door to the circulation of our message of Peace through that paper. I wrote therefore a preparatory article, in which I touched only such matters as that sect of adventurists could bear. And that my article was published in that paper. But when I offered the second article which touched nearer the Millerites' absurdities and follies, expecting Christ on the clouds and other paraphernalia, he refused to publish it, and is yet deceiving his disciples, although in the year 1840 opportunity was given to Millerites, to come out from their dreadful delusion. Whether Joshuah Himes was the first who misrepresented in so dreadful a manner our messsage, or Noyse perverted what the other deceiver published, they may decide; because the other is also a dreadful deceiver, who had opportunity to communicate to his readers our disclosures concerning Christ's Coming, but he refused to publish our article. But to the conclusion of this treatise Noyse belongs.

On the 5th of January, 1837, at 5 o'clock P. M. I received from a Heavenly messenger the order to prepare for starting to America. But at that time I did not know more than that in this country preparations were to be made for establishing the promised peaceable reign of Christ on earth. But my extraordinary mission commenced to be made manifest after the events which happened A. D. 1838 in connexion with my mission and which are explained in my above mentioned three German volumes. Instead of having studied those volumes and then reported accordingly, there came such ambassadors of darkness as we have here a specimen of John H. Noyse. Greater impudence could not be expected than to write about me without having studied my books in which I have published what should have been translated from the German also in other languages. In the third volume it is shown, where Swedenborg, Wm. Miller and others stand, who wrote before me on the second Coming of Christ. But before I undertook to write about their standing, I read their books; then I have shown, how parties and sects, each in their own way have given testimony to our mission. The principal of those parties have been mentioned in my third volume, which was published A. D. 1840. But John H. Noyse and his sect were not at that time so famous as to having been brought to my notice. At length a "noise" of his existence came to me in the following manner:

About the year 1844, while I had business in New York, Theophilus Gates came to me after having read an address of mine in which I urged readers to co-operate for establishing a centre of our work. T. Gates spoke about a certain point persuading me to adopt it for a sure success in establishing our centre. I said, that I did not know, whether I undestood him correctly or not. Therefore I would read if he had published anything on that subject and then I would talk with him about it. Then he brought to me his pamphlet, entitled: "the Battle Axe," in which he endeavored to prove "the free love doctrine" by the Bible as well as by authorities of this time. His greatest authority was a letter of this same John H. Noyse.

I gave a great lesson to Th. Gates who was ruining people by his infernal doctrine; but he did not digest my lesson. Then I made acquaintance with some John H. Noyse's disciples and asked them, how their leader became so blind as to support the damnable doctrine which opens the door to all kinds of lasciviousness, adultery and fornication, which ruins people and is diametrically opposed to the spirit of the New Testament. His disciples said, that he wrote that letter in a haste, and that it was published against his intention, and that he retracted his view expressed in that letter. Then I attended a meeting of Perfectionists in Newark, N. J. Some of them were with Noyse, others were against his supporting the Free Love doctrine. I addressed the audience. Then I was invited to dinner by a Perfectionist who did not belong to Noyse's Party. I was asked by my host, whether I did read or not, what appeared shortly before that in Noyse's "Perfectionist" against me. After my negative answer he gave me the number containing Noyse's article against me. I took it to the meeting which was appointed on the same Sunday afternoon and read that article at the meeting and explained Noyse's misrepresentations of the contents of my article to which reference was made in Noyse's article, and remarked that it was possible, that Mr. Noyse did not make purposely but only in haste those misrepresentations, and that in the case that he is a friend of Truth, he would retract what he had published misrepresenting my statements. I added, that in this case I would like to see him and converse personally with him about the matter. One of his disciples said. that Noyse was a man ready to receive truth, and that he wished to go with me to Mr. Noyse and to bear travelling expenses. We started and took also another friend of Mr. Noyse with us. At our arrival we were cordially received, till Mr. Noyse heard my name. At that moment he was entirely changed, took his friends into his room, while I remained on the porch. He spoke with them so loud, that I heard every word, while he reproached to them, that they took me with them. It was nearly dinner time, and I found proper not to speak about our case, till we would be together in his Printing Office. It happened soon after dinner. I said that those who were present, were Mr. Noyse's friends, but that I expected, that they were for truth, and that also Noyse will correct the errors and misrepresentations which he has published regarding my mission and regarding my statements in my article, to which he had reference in his article. But Mr. Noyse pertinaciously denied to have misrepresented my statements. I had in my pocket the number of the paper containing my article and that number of the Perfectionist in which my publication has been misrepresented. I read corresponding passages from both, and asked the witnesses, whether Noyse's report contained the same sense as my report. All his friends remained silent ; but he continued to be obdurate, and repeated in the most impudent manner, that he did not misrepresent my statements. I did know nothing until yesterday about his having misrepresented as early as 1840 my doctrine regarding Christ's coming and slandered and calumniated me already in that year. And when I met four or five years after that personally with him in his Printing Office about our business, he appeared as the most stubborn infallible Pope, affirming with the most impudent affront, that what he published against me, was true. But some bystanders commenced to cry : "Snake! snake! snake!" pointing out of the door of the Printing Office in a distance from the door to see what it was. There was a very large snake marching from a distance directly towards us and towards the door of the Printing Office, and went, in spite of the men gazing it, under the threshold, and sheltered its self under the floor of the Printing Office. It was most singular, that the devil, that means calumniator, by whom the snake was possessed, magnetized so the witnesses, that none of them took an instrument to kill the snake, although he could have easily reached one for this purpose in the Printing Office. After having been all so baffled, I said to Mr. Noyse, that the snake or the dragon is the Holy Ghost who comes from the depth of his Printing Office and inspires his readers with such infernal delusion, as appeared in his "Perfectionist" against my mission, and I left directly his place.

The man who has brought me to Mr. Noyse, left soon after that spectacle his own wife, a good natured woman, and went with another "Lady" to unknown regions. And Noyse left, not long after that that place, and founded in the State of New York, the Oneida community, in which his followers professed publicly and published their Free Love doctrine, and put it in practice in that community and elsewhere, when they had opportunity to deceive and ruin the incautious, abusing the Bible in the most horrible manner and anathematizing the true messengers of God. Such imposters must also give testimony to our mission in a manner convenient to their position, as I have given at the close of this treatise some hints, although I could write a volume of memorable events connected with John H. Noyse's "Perfectionist" and confirming the given hints. But this treatise being already weighty, we do not need to add an explanation, why our leaders were pleased to furnish Noyse's pamphlet to give occasion to these solemn warnings with which we close this treatise, which should be thankfully received from our directors by all parties and especially by Abolitionists and Republicans and by all kinds of Perfectionists and Spiritualists of the last fashion, who are by the abomination, called Free Love, so stupified, that they cannot comprehend our message, although they pretend to be Reformers. But those who will become true Reformers, must come on our ground according to the plan made public in the last treatise of this book by your sincere brother Andrew B. Smolnikar," extraordinary Ambassador" for the introduction of the New Era of Harmony and Peace.

THIRD TREATISE.

"The War in Europe, its remote and recent causes" in connexion with our Epistle to the Bishops of Illyria, to be communicated to the Emperors of Austria and France for the resurrection of the mortals as well as their departed friends from their misery and distress into the state of true happiness.

Instead of the treatise which was prepared to occupy this place in this book, we write on the 4th day of July, 1859, a New Treatise, while others are keeping the shadow for reality, rejoicing in companies and filling my ears with explosions of crackers and thunders of guns and my nostrils with the most disagreeable smell of gun powder, while I am mourning in my solitude in the midst of hundreds of thousands of people of the City of New York and neighbourhood, because they would not receive our message of peace and learn how to bring forth fruits of the true liberty of nations. This treatise was occasioned by the book "The War in Europe, its remote and recent causes" written by J. H. Duganne, and published a few days ago by R. M. DeWitt, Nassau St., No. 60, New York. I mention it here, because it contains a collection of facts and events, by the perusal of which any body, if he reflects upon what he reads, may be aware of what we continuously repeat, that people and their political and ecclesiastical governments have apostatized from Truth and Justice, and cannot establish the promised peace, except according to the plan which is given in the fifth or last treatise of this book. The causes of Revolutions and Wars and manifold other plagues are contained in the apostasy of men from Truth and Righteousness. This apostasy brings mortal men into the association with departed deluding and destroying spirits, as you know, if you have comprehended the preceding treatises, and you will receive the more proof of this important truth, the farther you will proceed in studying this book. Mortal men are in close connexion with congenial departed spirits. The life of man in his mortal body is a manifestation of influence from the sphere of spirits, for whose society he is prepared. By them he is moved and supported for action; they influence those who are congenial with them.

But men, if they are not versed in the inner life, are not aware of this influence; although this is the first and most necessary knowledge for the abolition of revolutions and wars and manifold other plagues, which originate from the influence of destroying spirits, who themselves may be so ignorant, that the magnetic fluid which they communicate to men is pestilential, as a man who is infected with one or the other kind of plague, may be ignorant of his dreadful condition, and of the fact that he infects also others who, in their ignorance of matters, are united with his deleterious condition. If, for instance, the Emperors of Austria and France, and their Generals and other Officers, and all who sympathize with one or the other, and contribute their share for the destruction of the enemy, would know the proper condition of spirits with whom they are associated and by whom they are inspired in their destructive work, they would be exceedingly frightened, and would cry: " What shall we do to be saved?

Many years before I knew anything about my present mission, I was aware by comparing the reports of the Bible with the reports of other ancient and modern works and with our own experience in regard to the spirit world, that angels and demons in the Bible are departed men and women of different high and low spheres, made manifest to men in mortal bodies, when there was suitable to give to men tangible testimonies, that mortals are in close connexion with departed congenial spirits. The legion, for instance, in the fifth chapter of Mark, is a legion or regiment of soldiers who have been destroyed in a battle. The captain and his legion had the grave or the cave in which dead bodies were located, for a suitable location to their degraded condition; and the magnetic fluid, which they inhaled into their inner or magnetic bodies which are used by spirits, came from the decomposed and rotten cadavers, and was the most delicious influence which they could communicate to their worshipers, and their captain has shewn his terrible madness by the attacks upon his medium, while he was compelled to make manifest, what he really was. But when he was not compelled to show his real condition, he was deceiving in like manner, as now departed Emperors, Kings, Generals and other warlike spirits are deceiving, till they bring their worshippers on the battlefield, where they effect such carnages, as we read now many reports in newspapers. In this madness the victors and their bishops and priests are feasting and singing " Te Deum," while the defeated are praying for the reverse, and neither party are prepared to reflect upon the crimes which they have committed by having killed their fellow men, who should have been educated and should have progressed in knowledge of truth and practice of virtue as long as their constitutions by applying the right means for the support of their physical strength and health, would have admitted. But alas! they have been wantonly killed, when they were least prepared for Heaven and best disposed for the infernal regions! And others have been mangled and wounded, so that they are crippled for all their lifetime and also hindered in the right use of their intellectual and moral faculties. And all who were drilled for war, were instead of progressing in virtue, retrogressing into corruption. Volumes oould be wrirten on this point of the deepest humiliation of the human race. Which are" the remote and recent causes of the war in Europe ?" The book which occasioned this treatise, contains a series of most detestable facts and proceedings as forerunners of the eruption of the volcanoes of the infernal furies which are destroying now in the wholesale human life and property ; because governments and nations are not in truth, but in delusion and confusion, the necessary consequence of which is destruction. Truth will make you free. This is the teaching of the master whose religion the belligerent parties profess with words, while their actions are instigated by the infernal furies. Also this book contains superabundance of testimonies of our mission, which is expressed on the title page. In my five German volumes published within the years 1838 and 1842, the mystery of iniquity of all governments which profess to be christian governments, has been disclosed, and their highest duty has been made evident to abolish those abominations and to unite with us for the introduction of Christ's reign, which will be the universal Republic of Truth and Justice, Harmony and Peace on the whole globe. In those volumes as well as in all my following publications it is made evident, that Peace can never be established on the globe in the present course of political and ecclesiastical affairs, and that, what they call peace, is only an armistice, during which the dragon and his host are inspiring the governments to amass means for new eruptions of revolutions and wars. The book which occasioned this treatise, contains a collection of testimonies confirming and illustrating our teaching, that true peace cannot be established, till governments and nations arrive on our ground. If the Emperor of Austria would evacuate this moment all places which he occupies in Italy, and if the Emperor of France and his allies would have in sincerity no other object in view, but the only one to make Italy perfectly free, I mean to make Italy a true Republic, and would sacrifice all their strength and influence to this only object, they could not realize their object, till they would learn and receive our message of Peace and adopt the plan given in this book for the introduction of the promised New Era. As long as they neglect to do this, they remain under the influence of deluding and destroying spirits. But these their masters are so controlled by our leaders, that when the measure of crimes of governments and nations is again and again filled, new eruptions of destructive revolutions and wars take place on such days and under such circumstances, that by our explanations of correspondences they become peculiar warnings; as we have already given specimens of this kind also in this book; and many more will be given on suitable places of the following pages. Readers should not forget that we are preparing them for the Epistle to the Bishops of Illyria.

Before we commence to translate that epistle, we must give a brief epitome of the contents of the treatise, which was to be printed in lieu of this treatise, and to which reference has been made in the preceding treatise, and we must write on this 4th of July, 1859 in the midst of great noise and continuous cracking and thunder of guns and so much smell of powder, that it becomes very tedious. This morning it appeared in newspapers, that Samuel Jackson's pyrotechnical establishment on 10th and Reed Streets in Philadelphia was yesderday afternoon destroyed by the explosion of fireworks, which were prepared for the exhibition on this day; but they yesterday burned Mr. Beck to death. We mention this case, because we saw it besides many other cases amongst the news of this day, and this Jackson is one of the many strong mediums of destroying spirits whom we endeavored many years ago to deliver from those spirits ; but they continue to prepare tremendous fireworks. In the octava of the outbreak of the infernal furies in the French Revolution of February, 1848, spirits commenced to awaken materialists by raps through the Fox Girls in the vicinity of Rochester of this State of New-York. They became at length generally known as Rochester Rapping Spirits ; because in the City of Rochester people first commenced to assemble in large numbers and hear those rappings, or also carefully to investigate, whether those raps came, as they purported, from spirits or from some other cause. As soon as I read in newspapers the reports of those manifestations, I understood the correspondences and also, why our leaders let the infernal powers exhibit their craft in this manner. Deluding and destroying spirits from the same spheres from which they have inspired their fighting mediums in Europe, commenced to give testimony in this country that there is truly such a relation between the living in the mortal bodies and the departed as has been disclosed in our publications, and at the same time also to show how they were duping and deluding such as would not hear our explanations regarding the true condition of spirits, but were quite pleasing with the answers which they received through the daughters of Mr. Fox and other mediums who commenced then to be developed in large numbers, that is, deluding and destroying spirits or infernal demons shewed by manifold perceivable possessions, that they were closely attached to congenial men and women. I made use of that opportunity and assured citizens of the United States, that rapping spirits would be dreadful destroying spirits also in this country, if their operations will not be stopped by the application of the means which are comprehended in our message of Peace. But I did not try those spirits in circles of spiritualists, till I received order from my leaders to do so. Opportunity was given in Pittsburgh, Pa. by the reports published in some English and German newspapers regarding the mediumship of

Christina Beil, (as the name of that medium of German parents is correctly written, but English reporters wrote it Beail, although it is the German Beil, that means a hatchet or axe. Her mediumship aroused a general attention, and while crowds of attendants were convinced that raps by which questions were answered, were produced by spirits, sceptics denied it, and Mrs. Swisshelm published in her "Saturday Visitor" the results of her investigations of spirit rappers at Christina Beil's mediumship. She thought, that raps must have been produced by some trick of one or the other mortal, although she was not able to discover the trick. The same confession was made in German newspapers by a German Lutheran Pastor. The excitement moved a skilful German chemist who was also a strong materialist, to investigate the matter in the expectation, that he might find out the trick. But he was sincere and confessed, that raps purporting to come from spirits, were produced by beings who understood the questions. But under the circumstances of his investigations they could not be produced by mortal men, and must have been produced by invisible agents.

A few days before my reading of those reports, a rapping spirit had been shown to me in an extraordinary manner, to relate which in this epitome there is no room. But by that manifestation I was instructed, that I should try the rapping spirits of Christiana Beil in the presence of sufficient witnessss. The same German learned chemist, and a German Pastor of the Reformed Church and other witnesses were present, when I tried the spirits of Christina Beil. Also that pastor belonged to that school of theologians who send their departed into such an eternity, from whence there is no return to mortal men. Such folly is according to our knowledge of the condition of the departed most pitiful materialism in disguise. But at our meeting with that medium in the house of her mother, soon a number of rappers commenced to show by raps in a number of places of the room, that they were ready to give answers to our questions. The medium commenced to ask, and instantly all others became silent, and the strongest amongst them gave answers with raps. To the question with whom he wished to converse, the pastor was shown by strong raps as the person with whom the spirit wished to converse, and he signified by raps also that he was ready to give his name by pointing out the letters of his name with raps. The pastor repeated the alphabet, and was quite astonished, that the letters spelled the name of his peculiar friend, a medical doctor and open materialist, who was expressedly denying man's immortality while he was in his mortal body, from which he departed a few months before that meeting. The pastor gave a number of questions, and expected to get some answer, with which he would be able to show, that such an answer could not come from that doctor. But at length the pastor confessed, that by nobody else except by that departed doctor he would expect all those answers which he had received.

When all was done which would convince the greatest sceptic, if he was prepared to reflect upon the facts, I interfered and remarked, that after having received sufficient testimony from that spirit, we wished to converse with some other, if any is present. Soon raps were heard of so differ ent a sound from the former, that any observer could perceive the exchange of spirits. The first gave answers to German questions; therefore also the second was asked, whether he wished to converse in German. He answered in the negative, and the medium was pointed out by raps as the person with whom he wished to converse. Then English questions were given and he consented to give his name. The alphabet was repeated, till all the letters of his name were pointed out by raps. And his name alarmed the medium exceedingly, that she commenced to cry, and also all her acquaintances were very much excited. I asked the reason, and was told, that that spirit was expected amongst the first when that girl became a medium, but they had never any test that he was present, and that they gave up all their hopes of getting any answer from him. Therefore his manifestation was so unexpected, that it produced such an effect upon the medium. I understood the whole matter. That spirit was the principal guardian of that medium or she was principally possessed by him, and he had rapped generally in the name of others, when the inquirers were so congenial with the medium, that he could look into their wishes. But he did not give his name, that he might not be discovered as the deceiver who rapped in the name of others. At length I came in the charge of my mission in March, 1851. I was acquainted several years before that with that pastor and exhorted him to study my books and then to proclaim our message of Peace. But my message was not popular and it teaches, that the belief of the close connexion of men in mortal bodies with congenial departed spirits is the A B C, to arrive gradually to a deep knowledge of true religion and to the true freedom and deliverance from lying destroying spirits. But pastors who became materialists, were scared when they perceived, that mymessage presupposes the close connexion with congenial departed. At length mediums or possessed by departed spirits alarmed the materialistic pastors. The mother of the medium belonged to the congregation of that pastorand she invited that pastor to come and be a witness. My leaders were controlling the legion of spirits, who came from different quarters with their witnesses, and in those circumstances the medical doctor Reitz, a peculiar friend of that pastor, was the strong rapper and the next was the lying spirit who, when there was no stronger than he, rapped in the name of others, till he was at length in our presence compelled to give his name. After that remarkable trial of spirits, I said to the pastor, that he should instruct the trustees of his church, to give me permission to deliver some lectures in that church and to explain that of which he was a witness, but which he could not understand in the connexion of things, in which it must be understood for the commencement of the New Era, which according to the testimonies given in his congregation, should be powerfully proclaimed from his church. But the pastor thoughtthat his congregation were not prepared for so deep things. Although I insisted, that I would make them very popular in the German language, which was the language of his congregation, and that it was his highest duty to make use of the opportunity to learn what is most necessary for Harmony and Peace of nations, he remained as obstinate as other Roman Catholic and Protestant Pastors.

Then I wrote an article for newspapers, in which I have shown what should be generally known regarding the spirit manifestations which commenced with raps by the mediumship of the Fox Girls to delude, as cunning foxes are accustomed to delude, such as would not receive truth which was disclosed in our message, and were discovered, when they were tried according to our mission at the medium Christina Beil's, which means the christian hatchet or the christian axe, an instrument for destruction, that they were deluding and destroying spirits, by whose influence destruction of life and property will continue until it will be stopped by receiving and spreading our message of Peace. That article was prepared in English and in German ; but editors who have spread deceiving reports regarding spiritualism, refused to publish my article. I sent it then to Boston, to be published there in a paper of spiritualists. But it was not popular and could not be published. Matters were to arrive so far as those will find them, who study and comprehend this whole book.

After that trial of spirits I returned several times to Pittsburgh and paid always my visit to that learned chemist, who was converted from a materialist into an enthusiastic spiritualist. He, like many others, was expecting through his mediums to receive truth regarding the spirit world. But he was offended, when I endeavored to make him comprehend, that those spirits with whom he came in communication by his mediums, were materialistic spirits who did not speak through his mediums from the miserable condition of their inner life but from the surface of their outward condition as they while in their mortal bodies were accustomed to boast, and to cheat and delude their fellow men. In the treatise which would have occupied this place, if I had not been moved to prepare this for the celebration of the 4th of July, 1859, and its octava, that people might commence to learn, how they could become independent from the invisible and visible tyrants by whom they are now enslaved, and inspired for revolutions, wars and other crimes, I have explained some very important spirit manifestations at my meetings with the learned chemist in Pittsburgh as preparations to the spirit manifestations which took place at my last visit to the City of Boston and neighborhood, and which constitute the principal part of that treatise, the publiaction of the whole of which must be delayed, and we give here in a synopsis as preparation to our Epistle to the Bishops of Illyria, the following items:

Boston is the City, in the cathedral Church of which by our mediumship A. D. 1838, such spirit manifestations took place, by which we have received the key to open the door for the promised New Era of Harmony and Peace on earth. We will give in the next following treatise of this book some light on those manifestations. But when our disclosures on those manifestations had not been received, at length spiritualism of the last fashion gained a peculiar stronghold in Boston, although materialism made great exertions to check also the modern fashion of spiritualism. Since A. D. 1838 I returned several times to Boston, and was trying to move some influential men or congregations for an examination of our message and of the credentials of our mission. When I arrived at the end of October, 1858, again in Boston I attended on the next sunday the conference of spiritualists, which was at that time on Sundays usually held in Boston. As soon as they finished their ceremonies by which their conference was opened, I found proper to speak a little in my Illyrian mother tongue, to arouse the attention to what I spoke then in English, and in the English language I rebuked materialists and testified our mission to restore true spiritualism. After my speech a medium arose, whom I did not know, but found out afterwards, that he was Agent of the Fountain House, where spiritualists had their resort and their speculations. He was rebuking a lecturer who was opposed to spiritualism, and, as I understood from the rebuke, misrepresenting facts, and came to that conference to expose spiritualism from his materialistic position, denying any manifestation from the departed. During that rebuke, for a proof, that spirits manifest themselves, he invited that lecturer and other materialists to a meeting, in which he offered to give an exact description of my mother whom he affirmed to have seen standing on my side, while I was speaking in the conference, and that although I was a perfect stranger to him, he was certain that she was my mother, and that he would give an exact description of her, so that he was confident, that I would confirm his description. There were spiritualists in the Conference who knew me, that I troubled them in the Utica Convention and elsewhere, and they seemed not to be favorable to that proposition.

On the next following Sunday I made again an attempt in said Conference to find out, whether there was any influential person amongst them ready to take an active interest in examining our message and the credentials of our mission. I commenced to speak from the point which was mentioned in the last conference by the medium testifying, that he saw my departed mother standing in her glory on my side while I was speaking. But I made the remark that I had two mothers in the spirit world, to wit, my first mother by whom I was born. She had great care during her life for my welfare, and having been a great medium of spirit manifestations before her departure, always anxious to know truth and act accordingly, she progressed with me also after her departure and became one of those my guardians, who take care for my provisions and protection against danger. In this her care she found a strong medium of spirit manifestations, an aged lady who was looking for the third angel, Revel. xiv : 9, because according to the testimonies which she had received, she was certain, that since A. D. 1836 he was preparing somewhat, and while she was looking for him since that year in Europe, she was directed by her guardian to America with the assurance that she would find him in this country. At length she heard one of my German lectures and comprehended, that I had the mission of the third angel. When she commenced to testify this, my mother appeared to her and entrusted her the care, which she herself had for me before her departure. My mother was an Illyrian, but this new mother was a German. Whenever I had opportunity to stop and write in her house, great spirit manifestations occurred. At length also she departed and is acting amongst the women who have amongst the departed peculiar offices for the introduction of the New Era. When I mentioned in said Conference somewhat about these matters and understood from the speeches of others that their spirits were drawing the audience in other directions, I turned also to other places, and tried besides others those professors at Cambridge, Mass. who were appointed A. D. 1857 as a committee to investigate the physical phenomena which were believed by some to have been caused by spirits, while others attributed them to other causes, and those professors, after having performed their investigations, published their opinion that spirits had nothing to do with the phenomena which they had investigated.

When I read that publication, I saw that readers, by the authority of those professors, were strengthened in materialism. Therefore, at my return to Boston I felt it to be my duty to try to move those professors of Cambridge from their materialism. I saw personally those three, who belonged to the committee who have publised their opinion regarding the phenomena, called spirit manifestations, and also the fourth who did not belong to the committee, but was the strongest operator to explode the truth, that departed spirits are in close connexion with congenial mortals, and that they, when circumstances are favorable and it agrees with the Plan of Divine Government, give also to exterior senses of men perceivable proofs of this connexion. I said to them, that A. D. 1838 were greater spirit manifestations in the Roman Catholic Cathedral Church of Boston by my mediumship and the mediumship of 144 witnesses, than mortal men could expect. Whereas that catalogue of witnesses as well as the events which happened in connexion with our proceedings, have been published in my books, I could by the means of that catalogue in a short time convince the professors of the great Truth of close connexion and mutual influence between mortals and their congenial departed, and by the public testimony of the professors the pernicious influence of their report regarding the spiritual phenomena would be abolished, and the way for the circulation of our message of Peace would be opened. They should therefore appoint time and place to meet with me for this most important investigation of what departed spirits are able to effect through mortal men. With all my exertions to move the professors they remained obstinate sinners against the Holy Ghost who gave them opportunity to learn what is most important to correct the pernicious effect of their report and to cease to brutalize their students with their materialism. I started from Massachussets to New Hampshire, because in that State besides other spirit manifestations in Concord a Convention of those adventists was held, who besides other blasphemies of the living God and his Christ teach also, that man dies as a beast, but that when Christ comes on the clouds, he will awaken the righteous from death, but the wicked will be eternally annihilated. As all other pestilence which is spread in the Papal and in the Protestant sects is supported by the use and abuse of the Bible, likewise also these "annihilators" made their discoveries of the annihilation of the wicked by the means of the Bible. They are spread through the country and especially through the States of New England, and are only a branch of the dreadful materialism which has brought the human beings so on the surface of the matter, that they stifled the most needful knowledge regarding the spirit world. I warned all sects of Adventists as well as others, everywhere. At length I met in October, 1858, with a portion of the Adventist annihilators in a Conference in Providence of Rhode Island, and tried to convert them from their folly. But they were not ready to hear facts and then reflect upon them with a sound reason, to know man in his interior life.

There are different sects of the Adventist annihilators; but that same sect, with whom I met in Providence, have appointed for November, 1858, a Convention in Concord N. H. The appointment contained a general invitation, without confinement to their sect, and I thought that there might be an opportunity for me to find some investigating minds who would listen to our message of Peace. But when I commenced to speak in their Convention, and their Popes saw that there was danger for their spirit annihilation, they applied to the audience with their complaint, that they found in Providence, that I did not believe in Christ's coming on the clouds and annihilation of the wicked and am rather a kind of a spiritualist. Therefore if I would remain I had to be silent, or I had to leave the Hall. I replied, that in their circular was no confinement to their sect, but their invitation contained exactly the opportunity for the proclamation of our message. But the possessed Popes by spirits of delusion and destruction became fierce and enraged, and I found best to leave them in their hall. My leader showed me that I should return towards Boston. At my return I was trying spirits on several places. It is to be understood that volumes could be written, if I would explain what I mention in this synopsis preparatory to my Epistle which I have sent in my handwriting to the Bishops in Illyria to be communicated to the Emperors of Austria and France, and which is to be printed in this treatise, that it might reach monarchs and their agents in this book, if it should not have reached them in hand-writing. But the events which occupy the largest portion of the treatise which would have appeared here, if the celebration of the 4th of July had not moved me to write and publish this in lieu of the other, may be expressed in this epitome in the following sentences:

During my travelling I am most time walking on foot. While I was walking on foot from Linn, Mass. to Chelsea City, I found the tollgate keeper standing without occupation on the turnpike, and asked him for a direction to the strongest spiritualist in Chelsea City. He directed me to a merchant. He was not at home, and I asked his clerk, to give me directions to some other spiritualist. He put several on a paper, the first of whom was Mr. Mansfield, and I was impressed to go to him. I was quite a stranger and without asking about the occupation of this Mansfield, I asked only for a direction to his house. When I found it, I was told that Mansfield was at his office No. 3. Winter Street in Boston. Without asking, what his occupation was, I came at length on the 3d of December, 1858, into his office. When I was in his office, the portraits of the dead drawn by some entranced medium with whom I was personally acquainted, and other paraphernalia reminded me, that that must be the celebrated medium J. V. Mansfield, of whom I read in newspapers, that many sealed letters not only from different quarters of America but also from other parts of the Globe, were directed to departed acquaintancas of the writers, and answers were asked from the departed which he could not give also in the case, if he would read the letters. But answers were to be given without opening the letters, by him as writing medium of spirits. He had to return the letters without opening the seal, and to add the answers as written by his mediumship. While reading the reports regarding that medium, I thought to see him, when I would come again to Boston. But while I was in the first part of November, 1858, in Boston I did not remember this, and came at my return from New Hampshire in the briefly related manner on the third December, 1858, against all my expectation to him. I think that he was present at the two above mentioned Conferences in Boston, in which I spoke before starting for New Hampshire. When I conversed on the 3d of December with him in his office, he invited me to come on Saturday, December 4th 1858, to his office and from thence to ride with him to his house in Chelsea City and spend Sunday, December 5th, with him. I was impressed to do so. That Sunday was the second Sunday in Advent. On the 4th, after the arrival in his house we both were tired and went to bed at 10 o'clock P. M. I rested well, till I was awakened by a female departed spirit who was in great distress and entreated me to give her assistance to kill her hüsband. I understood it in a spiritual sense to stop the pernicious course of her husband, and promised her my assistance. As soon as I promised her my assistance my leaders took her in protection and they expelled at the same time the whole company of her task masters out of the room, and then from two places on the outside of the house, from which they were compelled to remove. After that spectacle, the detail of which here is not the place to explain, the clock struck four. From this circumstance I understood, that the scene commenced at three o'clock.

There are certain hours, according to our spirit language by numbers most convenient for certain communications. As the communication requires, also the hour is selelected by my leaders in which they draw me into the inner state in which they show me, what is congruous to my mission. They put me, in that instance, from my sleep into the inner state of knowledge of what was going on. In this state I heard the female voice, entreating my assistance, but I did not see the female, although I was conscious, that she was surrounded by enemies of her happiness. The whole scene and explanation belonging to the treatise which will be published in an other time, these hints may suffice, to understand the following items. As sōon as I saw after that scene Mr. Mansfield and his wife at breakfast, I told them that I had a great spirit manifestation, which Mr. Mansfield could not understand, except if he would study some of my writings to know somewhat about my mission He read and I explained the substance of some points in my writings to make him known somewhat about my mission. Afternoon, while reading one of my pamphlets, he started suddenly and went very fast into another room, and brought directly some paper, put it on the table and said, that while he was reading my pamphlet, a spirit was impressing him to ask me to write questions which he would answer. I knew not who the woman was, who asked at three o'clock in the morning of that day my assistance to kill her husband, but I understood, that if I would follow the direction of my leader, he would reveal it in due time, I knew, that at that spirit battle, at which that female was taken under the protection of our leaders, the principal champion was the martyr John George Zeigler, an American of German descent, who in his mortal body studied deeper than any other man, my five German volumes, and forsook then all for our holy mission. While he was travelling in a steamboat he was pushed into the Ohio River by an enemy of our holy mission, and departed into the spirit world, in which he received such offices as he was most qualified for them. He having been the principal amongst those who took the woman in protection, while she asked my assistance, I thought, that if I would write to him questions, I would receive the information, who that woman was. It is to be understood, that Mr. Mansfield wished, that I should write so, that he could not see what I wrote, and then to wrap my writing, to which the spirit had to give answers. But I thought I could write in German, because I was certain that Mr. Mansfield could not read German. Therefore I said to Mr. Mansfield, that I determined to write in the German language to the spirit whom I had in my mind, to whom while he was a mortal, I wrote sometimes in German, sometimes in English, but he answered always my letters in English, and he, if he is present, will answer also through you in English. But Mr. Mansfield remarked, that I should write my questions in English, that he had lately great troubles with questions which have been sent by Otto Kunz from Pittsburgh in the German language to his departed, and that the last number of the Spirit Age contained an article of Otto Kunz in this respect. I remarked, that I was acquainted with Otto Kunz, (he is the learned chemist, by whom I was preparing my way in this treatise, for what follows) but that I did not hear anything about him for a long time, (to wit, since the summer of 1856, when I saw him the last time before my meeting with Mr. Mansfield). I added that I should like to see, what Otto Kunz had published. He brought then from an other room the number of the Spiritual Age, which has the date December 4th 1859. It must be added, that I had not before looked into that number, nor heard anything about Otto Kunz's article. But when Mr. Mansfield handed me that number, I read Mr. Kunz's article laid the paper on the table and said to Mr. Mansfield : I will write in English to the spirit whom I have in my mind. I had yet John George Zeigler in my mind; but when I took the pencil, I was impressed to write to Charlotte Kunz (the departed wife of Otto Kunz) in English, in the supposition, that she could not write English, while she was a mortal, and that also in the spirit world she did not learn to write English, that therefore to my English address we must receive some unexpected disclosures. I wrote therefore while the medium Mr. Mansfield turned in the opposite direction, that he could not see, what I wrote : " Charlotte Kunz, if you are present, please to write what you find proper." I folded my writing, that Mansfield could not see it. He was soon entranced, and gave the signs, from which I understood, that she was the person who asked at 3 o'clock A. M, my assistance, and then the communication was written by Mr. Mansfield in a correct English style and correct orthography and signed " Charlotte Kunz." The communication contains characteristic marks, that the controlling spirit was intimately connected with deep mysteries explained in my German books, but that he was not the writer, but one of the company belonging to J. V. Mansfield's guardians, wrote through him according to the wishes of Charlotte Kunz, but wrote so, as if she herself had written, After the communication directed to me has been written, and Mr. Mansfield reduced into his normal state, I requested him, to copy the communication, and to give the original and the copy to me; because I was asked in the communication by Charlotte Kunz, professing that she was the writer, that I might write to her husband. The handwriting of the copy was different from the original. I preserved the copy and sent the original to Otto Kunz, with my handwriting, remarking, that that communication has been produced by his wife under the assistance of our leaders, that he, Otto Kunz, might contribute his share for starting the centre of our Peace Union. I have quoted in my writings to Otto Kunz one of the characteristic notes testifying that the communication had certainly been produced under the assistance or control of my leaders. And that characteristic note had reference to Dante's Prophecy in the 33d Song of Purgatory. I speak of that prophecy in the Epistle to which we are preparing the way. I have explained also to Mr. Kunz several years before my meeting with his departed wife the substance of that prophecy. I thought, if he at the receipt of that unexpected communication would remember my explanation of that prophecy and other testimonies of my mission, he would not be too hasty in judging about what he could not understand in the communication but would expect my farther explanation regarding my communication; because the explanation could not be given in a letter, and he was also not prepared in those circumstances to study the treatise in which that communication is copied verbatim, and the preparation for its understanding and its explanation is given, and that treatise would have been published instead of this treatise, if we would not have prefered this in the expectation, that this might be more congruous to the present European War, which gives me opportunity to exhort nations and governments. And for this purpose, to communicate other important things in this treatise, we give only an epitome of the treatise which will be published in another convenient time. But Mr. Mansfield who has astonished many people in all quarters of the Globe by having given more than forty thousand answers to sealed letters directed to departed persons, became so remarkable, that he in connexion with the well known spiritualist Otto Kunz deserved a peculiar treatise, and appears also in this connexion of matters as a peculiar witness; because that which has been made evident in many cases in which we tried remarkable mediums, was in a peculiar manner confirmed, while we tried the spirits of J. V. Mansfield, to wit, that he has certain guardians by whom many are deluded, because those guardians give through him answers which are found correct, when they reach and control the writers of the sealed letters directed to their departed. But when this is not the case, answers are not correct. Mr. Mansfield told me, that the largest portion of his answers is correct. Such points in regard to the relations in which the departed have been with the inquirers are revealed in the answers, as Mr. Mansfield could not know them. From this circumstance is also explicable, how people could be so moved, that he had received many thousands of letters, although each applicant had to send one dollar fee to the medium, and three dollars in case of a guarantee that either an answer, if received would be sent, or the money returned. When we speak of correct statements in many cases, we add that in those communications was much of delusion regarding the spirit world. At length when the measure of abominations was filled, I had to try his spirits in the manner, the substance of which is given in this epitome, the treatise being prepared to be published, whenever a publisher is ready to publish a new book, which would contain that and other treatises. From that treatise it is evident, that when Otto Kunz wrote his letter to his departed wife and sent it to Mr. Mansfield to be answered by his mediumship, the tyrants by whom Mr. Mansfield is guarded, took her under their subjection. But to give in a new manner a most solemn warning to all spiritualists who will not progress on our ground, I was sent to Mansfield, and our guardians took under their control Charlotte Kunz and the spirits who are writing through Mr. Mansfield. The enemies of the truth, that departed spirits may use men as their writingmediums must explain the answers by assertions which in most cases appear most ridiculous, for instance, I heard the assertion, that Mansfield opens the letters. But he returns sealed letters as he receives them; although we would not deny the possibility of temptation to open one or the other letter of persons, with whom his guardians were not congenial, and therefore could not give an answer, But if I had shown to him my line directed to the departed Charlotte Kunz, although he has been before that in correspondence with her husband, Mr. Mansfield with all his guardians would not have been able to give the characteristic notes which are in the communication testifying, that some of our leaders was the superior, while J. V. Mansfield's guardian was writing that communication with Charlotte Kunz's signature, although there are the strongest marks in the communication, that she could not write it, but that a deluding and destroying guardian of J. V. Mansfield wrote it, partly according to her wishes, partly according to his own impulse, partly according to the dictation of our leader who controlled him, that he inserted the characteristic notes given by our leader. This is the epitome of that treatise, which was to be given in this treatise as a peculiar preparation to my epistle to the Bishops of Illyria. But before we commence to translate it, we must add also the following remarks. When our leaders compel in one place "the Secret Enemies of True Republicanism" to bring to daylight their abominations for our peculiar use to enlighten this degraded generation, they send us corresponding testimonies also from other places, and we have collected in said treatise some extraordinary testimonies for an illustration of the answers of the sealed letters by J. V. Mansfield's mediumship. A peculiar witness in this repect was Doctor Randolph, whose spirits I tried several years before my meeting with Mansfield; but he was not ready to be converted from darkness to the light which is kindled by our disclosures. At length when I tried Mansfield's spirits, newspapers commenced to publish Dr. Randolph's confessions. He tells: "I was a medium about eight years, during which time I made three thousand speeches," &c. "And to day I had rather seen the Cholera in my house than be a spiritual medium! for years I have lived alone for spiritualism and its cognates. Henceforth I live to combat many of the identical doctrines that I once accepted as Heavenly truths." "I enter the arena," says he "as the champion of common sense, against what in my soul I believe to be the most tremendous enemy of God, morals and religion, that ever found foothold on the earth---the most seductive, hence most dangerous form of sensualism that ever cursed a nation, age or people." If Dr. Randolph had been brought from spirits of delusion on our ground, he would have assisted us to open the door for the New Era. But he returned to the sects, from which spirits commenced to manifest themselves in their materialistic deluding manner, till we commenced to show, what they were, and then they commenced to be caught in their lies, and many spiritualists commenced to be scared; but they would not progress on our ground, and returned to professed materialism and sectarianism. But the concentration of all abominations of the perverted spiritualism is in the Papal Imperial Royal Courts. Many spirits delude monarchs and their supporters either openly by peculiar manifestations, or without such manifestations deceiving secretly monarchs and supporters, that they prepare at length for war and commence to fight in horrible battles, which is the highest manifestation of the infernal furies. That they might stop this abominable work in which they are now engaged, I wrote the following epistle, which I give in a free translation, and then I will add some remarks for a conclusion of this treatise. You will find in this epistle some repetitions of what has been mentioned in the first treatise of this book, because when they were setting that in type I did not think about writing this treatise in which what is repeated, should be repeated so often till it is comprehended.

The Epistle is entitled :

"Most important events for rulers of nations.

To P. T. Anthony Slomshek, Prince Bishop of Laibach.

Long Island, State of New-York, June 13th 1859.

Reverend Bishop! Being in occupations of my office on this anniversary of momentous events on this Island, I am impressed by the spirit who has brought me to America, to write again after a long interruption, to my native country, and to direct my Epistle to you, to communicate copies of it also to the bishops of Triest and Goricia. I asseverate before you, three witnesses, that I am not guilty of the blood which is shed in the present terrible war; although I would be most guilty, if I had not faithfully fulfilled the duties of my charge. If those to whom I have written at Vienna, in our native country, and also in other countries of Europe, had discharged as conscientiously the duties of their office, as I did those of my office, the promised universal peace would have been established not only in the whole of Europe, but also in other parts of the globe. But whereas there was deficiency in respect to the intellectual and moral preparations of those who were in the office, the terrible consequences therof are more and more visible. To bishops I write usually in Latin. But this epistle should be delivered by you to the government of Austria, and published to the nations not only in German, but also in as many other languages as possible.

Prince Bishop Anthony Slomshek! Having had more opportunity than others who are at present bishops under the Austrian government, to obtain knowledge about me during my residence in Europe and by wise providence having become a bishop of the diocese, in which I was born, educated and ordained a priest, I expect that you will receive light from the spirit, to comprehend correctly the hints which may be concentrated into the space of an ordinary epistle. You know that I had from my youth an extraordinary desire to search not only the Jewish and Christian but also the antiquities of other nations, and to compare the results of my investigations with what others have brought to light in former times and recently, to find out, how the promised universal peace will be established. After my having been six years secular priest of the diocese of Laibach, I entered the Benedictine Order of the Monastery of Saint Paul in Carinthia, for the purpose of obtaining more time and opportunity in that order which furnishes learned professors, than in my native country for a continuation of my investigations for the peace of nations. After my having searched two years in the library of the monastery, I became Professor of Biblical Literature in Clagenfurt, and in that city I became acquainted with you, you having been there Spiritual Adviser of Students of Divinity.

During the ten years of my Professorship I had opportunity to examine many points, which I would never have had oppertunity to examine in the Diocese of Laibach. But I did not know that the spirit who was my guide from my youth, was preparing me for the office which has been entrusted to me in America. Moreover, notwithstanding I had from my youth peculiar inclination to study the Bible and to read not only the writings of the Church Fathers but also the writings of the old Heathen and Jews for the purpose of getting more light on the Bible, during the last ten years of my Professorship I did not yet know that the office with which I am commissioned in America, had been manifoldly prophesied in the Bible, and the prophecy repeated by prophets of the christian centuries as well as in our time by images suitable to the seasons. Neither had I any thought to make a voyage to America, till the spirit of truth showed by evident testimonials, that he called me to this country. Then he opened also the way for me hither so wonderfully, that although the Prelate of the monastery of Saint Paul resisted with all his power, and the monks who were my friends, united with him to hinder my voyage, Emperor Ferdinand was enlightened to let me have my passport to America.

Signs and wonders preceded and accompanied my voyage to America, and I reached this continent first in Boston of the State of Massachussetts on my birth-day, November 29, 1837. In that city all that was required for the continuation of our work, has been so prepared by invisible agents, that although I had not the least foreboding to remain in that city, I became convinced by the signs which happened there, that in the Roman Catholic Cathedral Church in Boston important ocupations had been prepared for me. I did not yet know the particular occupations: but I followed faithfully the directions of the spirit and performed in that church all, that had been shown to be performed by me. On the 7th of January, 1838, one hundred and forty-four witnesses signed their names in my catalogue. Also those witnesses were guided by invisible agents in such a manner, that they, too, performed in that church, what was required of them, so that on Easter Sunday, April 15, 1838, in the Cathedral Church in Boston, in the presence of these 144 and many other witnesses by my instrumentality the solemn excommunication of the Beast with seven heads and ten horns from the Church of Christ has been performed, that is, solemn declaration has been made, that the mysteries which are contained in those figuritive expressions, do not belong to the Church of Christ and must be therefore abolished from the earth. A long chain of signs, according to the prophecies, preceded that excommunication, and signs succeeded and are continually repeated. By these signs our mission, that is, my mission and the mission of my fellow labourers has been confirmed, and the dreadful condition of those who are opposed to our action has been most evidently developed. In the years 1838 and 1839 the first two volumes of Memorable Events appeared in print. Those events took place in my experience for a testimony, that Christ appears by His messengers for the foundation of the promised peace on earth. A box of those volumes was sent to the Emperor of Austria, and my written explanation was given, that in my books the will of the most High Majesty has been made manifest, to whom Emperors and Kings are bound to submit and to learn to know the events which have been explained in my books and to become with us messengers of peace to the nations, and for this purpose to give my books to the best theologians for the strictest examination, that the result of their examination might be sent to me, to be published with my remarks, that nations might learn what is required for the foundation of the peace of the world. I assured the Emperor, that dreadful revolutions and wars will be the consequence if my advice will be rejected.

After having received no answer to my writings to the Emperor, to the parson of his court, to a number of bishops and other influential men of the Empire, and A. D. 1840, my third volume appeared, in which was shown, that the unexpected events which have been explained in the first and second volumes, happened according to prophecies, and would not have been unexpected to bishops, if they had studied prophecies and observed the signs of the times, and reflected upon the disclosures given by our forerunners upon these matters, I did not send that volume straightway to Austria, but I sent a box of all three volumes to the King of Bavaria, with a similar written warning to the King, as in the preceding year to the Emperor of Austria, and with the most urgent demand, that after the Emperor of Austria and his bishops had neglected to fulfil their highest duty, he should become the messenger of peace to all other monarchs and open the way to the circulation of our message. At the same time a copy of all three volumes was sent to the King of France with the most urgent written petition that he should order without delay a French translation of the three volumes to be spread everywhere in France, and our solemn assurence was added, that, if he neglects to fulfil this highest duty, Revolutions and Wars will be the necessary consequence of this neglect.

In an ordinary epistle farther hints cannot be given in regard to what was done on our side, to move the one or the other government to order the strictest examination of our message, which contains the means for obolition of all Revolutions and for the foundation of the universal peace on the whole globe ; but I remark, that when they would not hear our warning voice, Revolution broke out in February, 1848, under such preparatory, concomitant signs, and under such corresponding events, that after having studied those events in my writings which have been after that partly published in the English language partly preserved for publication, you will see, that, after our warnings given under Heavenly inspiration had been contemptuously rejected, the infernal furies had received the power, to commence to spread the flood of Revolution exactly on the same day, which gives the most evident testimony, that Revolution broke out according to a higher calculation on account of the contempt of our message of peace.

Emperor Ferdinand having been compelled by that Revolution to issue a constitution, I read that constitution in a newspaper on the 18th April, 1848, and was moved on the 19th April, which was the birth-day of the Emperor, to give him in consequence of my charge a written assurance that by that constitution the government and people will be saved from ruin, if the Emperor accepts my offer; because in this case I was ready, to start directly for Vienna, and show how the Free Press which was guarantied by the constitution, would be properly used for developing and spreading truth, as people have a right to demand, and its abuse impeded, as the government is bound to impede it. I have given the Emperor the assurance, that this, our offer, was made under higher direction for the true happiness of the Imperial Family and the people. I have sent in the same writing our proclamation to the nations of the empire, and exhorted the emperor, that if he would write to me, that I should come to Vienna, he should at the same time publish our proclamation in all languages of the empire; because, if he accomplishes this, by our use of the free press the door will be opened for the introduction of the promised peace of the world, but on the contrary revolutions and wars would be repeated and governments and nations ruined. Those highly momentous documents were sent to the minister of the Austrian government in Washington to be forwarded to the emperor. Informatian was given to the minister in my next letter, to which post office he should send the answer, if he should receive any for me from the Austrian government. After having thus notified him I have received no answer; but very important signs were given of the approaching war in which the emperor resigned the throne and Hungary was wasted.

The three monarchs to whom my books have been sent, but who have neglected to make use of the means contained therein for the peace of nations, have been compelled to give up their thrones, but nations could not become partakers of the promise of the universal peace; because it will not be established by the sword but by the means contained in our message of peace, and we have received so many signs according to prophecies as evidences of our mission, that whereas since the year I838 to 1842 five volumes have been written in this respect, I repeated while I was writing the fifth volume, that five hundred volumes could be written, if we would continue to explain prophecies of past ages and their development in the preparations for our mission and during our mission, and the signs by which our mission is confirmed. But we have explained superabundance of them, because by our explanation the dreadful condition of governments and nations has been disclosed. Signs continue steadily, although the blind leaders of the blind, while the Lord appears as a thief, comprehend them as little, as the Pharisees did, when Christ appeared and prophesied the destruction of the city and the temple.

Confined to a common letter, I can give only some hints. While the terrible war was raging principally in Hungary, I laboured industriously at the commencement of the year 1849 to move the American bishops, to appear either personally or to send their Theologians to a convention in the city of New York, to whom I offered to read in the Latin language my system for the abolition of revolutions and wars and introduction of the world's peace.

I did all I could to move the bishops to attend our Latin convention, and to make as many objections and remarks as they would find suitable, although all must have been made in writing and handed to me, to be annexed with my remarks to my system and published in Latin and in translations, that men everywhere, could learn our message of peace and all nations might become partakers of the greatest promises and the world's peace could be established.

After bishops had neglected their highest duty, I translated the Latin system into English and German, and made most urgent applications to several Presidents and to congressmen of the United States, to move the American government, to assemble a convention for the same object, for which I endeavoured to move bishops. In the meantime Lewis Kossuth arrived in America, and I considered it to be my peculiar duty, to make use of what was in my power, to direct him from the spirit of destruction to peace and to explain to him my system in which is shown, how without soldiers the rights of men will be restored and the peace of the world established. After several letters of preparation, at length I met personally with him in Cincinnati. But he was cunning and let me come to him in company with others, and when I required to speak privately with him, he excused himself with not having time to speak with me privately, and directed me to Count Pulski, who was his associate. I paid to this man several visits, and shewed to him that it was necessary for Kossuth and his assistants, to study my system and to retire with me for this purpose. But the result of all my labour was, that at length Kossuth had sent to me the message that it was impossible for him to give up his plan. He is a strong "Medium," as those are called here who are possessed, and those who are possessed by destroying spirits, have their work, to torment rulers or also to destroy them, if they will not find salvation in our message of peace.

Having here only opportunity to give hints on points, on which I could write volumes, I remark, that when the American government could not be moved to call a convention for an examination of our message of peace, I wrote, when Emperor Napoleon III. was preparing for war against Russia, to his ambassador in Washington, that the emperor would gather together the highest merits for himself and mankind, if he, instead of the war preparations against Russia, would call bishops of his empire to Paris, to examine with me my Latin system for the foundation of the world's peace. By doing this he would make himself and his friends and at the same time all nations happy ; but in the opposite course he would prepare misfortune for himself and France. I assured the ambassador of the French government in Washington, that if he before he would write to the emperor, himself wished to be convinced of my assertion, I was ready if he would call me, to come myself to Washington and to explain to him my system as long as would be necessary to convince him, that we have truly received from Heaven the commission and credentials for the foundation of the worlds peace, and that those regents will be in this and in the future life most unhappy, who refuse to accept our invitation. I have received no answer from the ambassador of the French government.

Although I am writing very closely in my advanced age without spectacles, which I never used in my life, I have very little space in a common letter, to mention also the following items: The nearer we were approaching to the present Revolutionary Wars in Europe the stronger were also the signs of warning, and they are building just now on the land which has been bought for our Peace-Union, a hall for our conventions, in which our system for the foundation of the world's peace will be explained and messengers of peace will be educated to be sent in all quarters of the world. But whereas, before their labors will establish the world's peace everywhere on the globe, all monarchs and their families might be exterminated, if they would not make use of the means for the foundation of the world's peace, I write this letter on this Feast of Pentecost and anniversary of momentous events. Your predecessor, Anthony Aloysy Wolf, Prince-Bishop of Laibach, was one of those Prince Wolves, who have received my first two volumes, but were not prepared to study them, and to proclaim to Emperor Ferdinand and to the nations, the great things which the Lord has done. Those wolves have deceived in regard to our mission the Emperor, the priests and the people, and by this deception they became the originators of all those murders, which have been perpetrated in revolutions and wars and manifold other manners, which would have been prevented by receiving and spreading our message of peace. These are the fruits, when wolves are made pastors of nations! By murders which are perpetrated in revolutions, wars and other ways, those who are murdered, are turned into infernal furies, instead of having been converted by suitable education, into Heavenly Angels. By these furies which have been murdered in revolutions and wars, nations which are now living, are instigated to murders in revolutions and wars and in manifold other manners and also to all kinds of other criminal deeds, the atmosphere is disturbed and men are tormented with all kinds of plagues, and if they are not murdered cruelly by force, their lives are shortened manifoldly, so that also those who live longest, would have lived much longer, if it would have been introduced amongst nations and duly used, what we know, but cannot use till governments introduce that which we demand.

I was Professor of Divinity in Babylon which is spoken of in the Revelation ; but whereas I was sincerely searching after truth for my own and the welfare of my fellow-men, matters have been disclosed to me, which I had never expected, while I was prepared without my knowledge by invisible agents for my present charge. According to this charge I am now Professor of Divinity or Church-Doctor for the promised peaceable Reign of God on Earth. As Church-doctor I will teach bishops and priests as well as monarchs and other grandees of the kingdoms of this world, when they will be ready to hear the Heavenly voice which is made manifest through so feeble an instrument as I am, how to pacify the furies into which men are converted by murders and how to draw them into the resurrection, that is, from their low to a higher condition. My apostolic name which I have obtained on the feast of the apostle Andrew, November 30, 1795, is Andrew. But when on the 30th November, 1826, at the solemn profession of the Benedictine order I adopted by higher impulse the name Bernardus, then also Pope Leo XII. was inspired, that he promulgated Bernardus a Church-doctor. He in his shortsightedness, had in his mind the celebrated monk of the twelth century. But neither that monk who was preaching crusades, nor Pope Leo XII. knew, that Turks, heretics and other nations will be converted in true christians without blood shedding and Christ's peaceable reign will be established on the whole earth. But the Pope spoke as prophet of our mission who was at that time High Priest and prophesied, that, whereas I adopted in the prophetical profession of the Benedictine Order the name Bernardus, I had to pass as monk through the last epoch of my studies of preparations for my present charge, till I became Doctor Ecclesiae, Church-Doctor, teaching what bishops and doctors of Divinity do not understand, although it is highly necessary for the peace of nations. From my first arrival in the Benedictine Order, when I determined to live there, till I started for America, exactly twelve years passed.

By the memorable events which happened in the Cathedral Church in Boston, a key was given us to unlock prophecies, which have been before either entirely locked, or only in some measure unlocked. Some interpreters have known, that the seven churches in the second and third chapters of the Revelation were prophetical churches, typifying the seven states, to which all churches of the christian name since the edition of the Revelation until the foundation of the universal peace on earth may be reduced, so that every portion of the christian name belongs to the one or the other of the seven churches. In the third of the above mentioned volumes, we, that is, I under the direction of invisible assistants, have disclosed so much regarding the fulfilment of the prophecies in our time, as is abundantly sufficient for testimony of our mission. In our disclosure Thyatira in the 18th verse of the second chapter of the Revelation is the type of the Roman Catholic Church. What is said concerning that church until the end of that chapter, you Bishops should at length consider and digest well. You kept fast what you did not understand, till at length the Lord comes by our mission, and unlocks by our mediumship the Divinity for His Reign of peace. We have overcome and to us was given "the Rod of Iron and the Morning Star." I speak in the name of all those who are co-operating with me according to the Plan of the Most High for the universal peace of all nations. We have "the iron rod," but not the iron sword. The iron rod is only a symbol of our office to announce judgments to the disobedient nations and to their rulers. They are bruised enough and broken. Those who remain, should at length hear our voice, then their wrong systems will be broken to pieces, but men will be saved. For we have received not only the iron rod, but also the morning star. In the great temptations through which we had to pass, we remembered the morning star which appeared several times during the sun shine in close connexion with our steps, and once in a peculiar connection with you, Prince Bishop Anthony Slomshek! as well as in connection with the Emperor of Austria! You remember that I wrote at a certain occasion my opinion in regard to your sermons which appeared in print in our Slavonian mother tongue, and in that my article I made also some extracts from my Latin manuscript, "On the congeniality of languuages," to publish them with that article in the "Carinthia. I finished writing that article on the 6th February, 1835. When I was on the 7th February well nigh ready to go to my students in the college, I was moved by the spirit to write instantly a prophetical conclusion to that article. When I finished that conclusion, I hurried to be in the college. After that there was much talking among the Professors nnd others about the morning star which appeared on that forenoon during sunshine. I explored exactly the time, and found that the star appeared, when I commenced writing that prophetical conclusion, and disappeared, when I finished writing. I handed then that article to you, to deliver it to the editor of the Carinthia. But there occured an accident, that the article appeared later than I expected, so in the Carinthia, that the last part with the great prophecy regarding the peace of nations was published on Easter Saturday April 18, 1835, or on the Eve of the birth-day of the Emperor Ferdinand the first year of his government. His birth day was celebrated that year on Easter Sunday. An exact calculation was made by our invisible agents. The poems of two panegyrists of the birthday of the Emperor appeared in the same number immediately before our prophecy. Those two adulators were types of the two adulators, Joseph Pletz Parson of the Imperial Court, and Anthony Alosy Wolf, Prince Bishop ot Laibach. These two prelates have deluded the Emperor in regard to our mission, and as a consequence terrible judgments came upon governments and nations. But this writing is connected with the Morning Star, which should be delivered by you to the young Emperor Francis Joseph and to many nations as well as the ancestors of the Emperor, who are waiting in the Empire of death for their redemption by our Message. It should be delivered by you in the midst of terrible judgments. If you have the spirit which I expect in you, you yourself will carry this letter without delay to the Emperor, and explain personally, what is necessary for his resurrection and strength. Now he belongs in the 16th verse of the 17th chapter of the REVELATION. Kossuth, Mazzini and other heroes of the Revolution are preparing the Harlot for Emperors and Kings, who are fulfilling the judgments which are announced in that verse. But we to, whom this victory is promised, belong to those, who are united with the lamb in the 14th verse of the 17th chapter of the REVELATION and will overcome the Beast and its ten horns. To wit, we have the chain, with which the Dragon, the seducing and destroying Serpent, will be bound and cast into the abyss, REVEL. xx: 2, That is the magnetic chain of events of past times in connexion with events of this time. In this chain the genuine condition of the existing political and ecclesiastical governments appears in its true light, so that, when this chain will be duly spread and made known to Nations, they will be carried from the existing Babylon into the New Jerusalem. Who ever amongst the rulers comprehends this and carries the people into the New Jerusalem, into the promised Reign of Peace, he himself and his family, as well as his departed or yet in mortal bodies living congenial relations will be brought into the true happiness; but on the contrary those rulers and who are attached to them, who despise our apostolic voice, will be exterminated. Judgement will not cease, till at length it destroys themselves also. I have given in this Epistle as many hints as are sufficient for such bishops who are not entirely dead, to believe, when I assure them, that in our writings it has been made clear and evident, that our chain or our system, which, for Peace of Nations, should be made known to all political and ecclesiastical Governments, is astronomically and historically correct. Therefore that of the three named bishops, who receives first this Epistle, should inform the other two of the matter and summon them to go directly with him to the Emperor. Who comprehends this, and is inspired by the Holy Ghost who is our director, for the accomplishment of Divine Decrees, is with us a messenger of God. He should as such appear before the Emperor with this Epistle, read to him the Epistle, and explain it, and summon the Emperor to become with us a messenger of God, and may he be seemingly in profit or seemingly in loss in regard to the Emperor Napoleon, to send this Epistle to Emperor Napoleon, and require instantly an armistic under the condition, that he is desirous to make immediately, with condescension, a treaty of Peace, to hear the "Messo di dio," the messenger of God, spoken of by the prophets of the Old and New Testament as well as by the prophets of the succeeding ages of the Christian Era, and to fulfil the will of the Most High for the welfare of nations. Amongst those prophecies is one of the most remarkable in the 33rd Song of Purgatory in the Divine Comedy of the great Italian Poet Dantè, in which the spirit Beatrice, Dante's departed wife, speaks of the "five hundred, ten and five messenger of God," that is, of "Smolnker messenger of God."

The number 500, 10 and 5, that is the number 515, is opposed to the number 666 in the Revelation, xiii: 18. The name which comprehends the mysteries which are contained in the 17th and 18th verses of the 13th chapter of the Revelation and also the number 666, has been delivered into our hands, and all that belongs to the name, has been explained in my books, in which to obtain the number 666, we had to write the name with Greek letters, because the Revelation appeared in the Greek language. And likewise also my name SMOLNKER, as it was originally exactly pronounced, to wit, with short *o* and short *e* must be written with Greek letters. This was the exact pronunciation of my name, as I heard it pronounced by my grandparents and my parents. And the Greek letters with short *o* and short *e* exactly pronounced in my name SMOLNKER, give exactly the number 515, which is the number of the messenger of God in Dante's prophecy. If you add this number to the year 1321, in which Dante died, you obtain the year 1836. "The messenger of God" is in the quoted prophecy the same as the 3d Angel in Revel. xiv. 9. That the third Angel regarding whom the prophecy commences in the 9th verse of the 14th chapter of the Revelation, had to appear before the public about the year 1836, and also that that Angel or messenger would not be a departed but a man living in his mortal body, has been shown in the last century by Doctor Bengel and his disciples using admirable astronomical calculations by the means of the prophetical numbers in the Revelation. My first German teacher, a Franciscan Monk from Bavaria, inserted the letter *i* into my name, and taught me to write my name SMOLNIKER, till at length Professor Valentine Vodnik wrote my name as I write it now. The numbers of my name, after having received those changes, if you calculate the years, commencing with Dante's death, give also highly important stopping points in the development of the mysteries of the Theology for Christ's peaceable reign. I can give in an epistle only some hints.

By many of our forerunners many points have received partial disclosures, or there have been prepared several links for the chain, with which we will strangle the Harlot and the Giant who sins with the Harlot, without hurting the flock and the fields, according to Dante's prophecy. This prophecy mentions also the stars by which our advent is announced, and in my books several apparitions of unexpected stars are remembered in close connection with our office. In Dante's prophecy is the messenger of God a collective name as well as the third Angel or messenger in the 9th verse of the 14th chapter of the Revelation. One man is representing the whole society by whom is accomplished what is comprehended in the prophecy. The representative had to execute and explain the mystery. At the expiration of the year 1836, which year has been so mysteriously announced by the prophets, that I knew nothing about it, I was called on the 5th day of January, 1837, at 5 o'clock p. m. to this office. The call was delivered to me by an Angel of the Lord, that I should make the resolution to prepare for my voyage to America. And when I said: "O Lord! Thy will be done!" the same moment a great light appeared over the City of Klagenfurt, where I was Professor of Biblical Literature and you were Spiritual Adviser in the Theological Seminary. You yourself have perhaps seen the light-ball, or certainly heard much and read in newspapers about it. I myself have not seen it, because I was in a deep trance and received at the same moment the order by a Heavenly messenger.

Here is no space to say more about Dante's prophecy. In my third volume of Memorable Events more than one hundred pages have been used for disclosing Dante's strange prophecy regarding the Messenger of God in the 33d or the last Song of Purgatory, in connection with other prophecies with which it is parallel and in connection with the prophecies which have been given A. D. 1814 at the first distribution of premiums after the fall of Emperor Napoleon I. when our city of Laibach returned under the Austrian government, and I received Dante's Divine Comedy for the first premium out of the Italian language. And whereas I am labouring since my arrival in America with the greatest zeal to save men and to bring them from Purgatory into Heaven, warlike spirits are murdering and casting them into hell. Yet I have great confidence that by your intermediation not only the Emperor of Austria but also the Emperor of France will hear the Heavenly voice, which is sounding in this letter. I have written several months before the outbreak of this war a book in the English language ("this same book from which we take away other manuscript and publish this epistle,") to publish it as soon as circumstances will be favourable. I have shown in that book by peculiar events which occurred with Emperor Louis Napoleon, but which are not comprehended by him and his mediums till they study to know our chain to bind the dragon, Revelation, xx: 2. that Emperor Napoleon is a very strong medium of destroying spirits, but that I foster the hope, that he will comprehend our message of peace and draw also his Uncle Nepoleon I. into our reign of peace and become a great apostle of peace to the nations.

Both Emperors, the Emperor of Austria as well as the Emperor of France, will become truly great if they accept our message of Peace, which contains the substance, that they should directly conclude Peace, with all mutual condescension and with our assurance, that soldiers who will not be needed in God's Reign of Peace on Earth, will obtain according to the plan which is to be published in the above mentioned book "(in this book)" and which after the English edition may be translated also in other languages, occupations most suitable to their strength and the best spiritual education, to be truly happy in their mortal bodies as well as after their departure,

But whereas no treaty of Peace can be of duration in our time, unless the governments enter into Christ's Peaceable Reign, which to establish we have obtained the mission, you, Prince Bishop Anthony Slomshek, and also the other two witnesses who are bound to give you all possible assistance, are particularly summoned to recommend most urgently to both emperors,as soon as they conclude an armistice and prepare the way to the treaty of Peace, to appoint also a healthy place, where according to the geographical situation and other circumstances bishops of both empires can easiest meet, for our Convention in which my Latin manuscript which should have been examined A. D. 1849 by the American Bishops in the Convention which was appointed in the City of New-York, is to be examined according to the same rules mentioned above, and to give me as well as the bishops information of this affair; because I am ready to do all in my power for the Peace of Nations. You, Bishop Anthony Slomshek are requested, to send me directly the result, after having received and read this letter in your Consistory, and direct your letter to

ANDREW B. SMOLNIKAR,

DONNALLY'S MILL, PERRY COUNTY,

Pennsylvania, in North America.

We cannot enter into explanations of the points mentioned in this Epistle to Bishop Anthony Slomshek. The substance of the remote and recent causes of the war in Europe and of the causes of all revolutions and wars is, that men are living on the surface, in materialism, according to their animal lusts and passions, using their reason to accomplish their animal desires, and neglecting the one thing needful to grow in the knowledge of their true inner condition and the true condition of the departed, and in corresponding virtue for high spheres of spirits to promote the true welfare of the whole human race while they are promoting their own welfare. The treasures which I collected from my early youth to this advanced age for the promotion of the common welfare, I carry with me into the spirit world. But those who, instead of having cultivated their inner man, came on the surface into the materialistic life, and lived according to their animal passions and carnal lusts and according to the custom of their party and sect, and supported blindly the performances contained in the traditions and systems which have been delivered to them by their predecessors, were preparing in their way for revolutions and wars, instead of having learned our disclosures that the time had arrived for the abolition of the Old Heavens and the Old Earth, that is, of the old ecclesiastical and political institutions, and how they are to be abolished in the most peaceable manner.

In this ignorance of things which have been disclosed in our publications, those who keep up those Institutions, come in collision with those who endeavour to destroy them without knowledge of their prophetical meaning and of the truth which is behind the vail of the outward form, and without preparation for a better state of human affairs. This collision is continuously preparing revolutions and wars. Men on the surface not knowing the right means for true liberty, use the means which destroy not only liberty, but also human life and property, and life is wantonly destroyed, because men in their dreadful degraded condition do not know how to appreciate it. In this condition, if the old systems would succeed so far as to crush down with absolute despotism all movements for deliverance, they could not keep for a long time people in bondage of absolutism. Crevices would be always found, from which the movements of the secret aspirations for liberty would commence to be made manifest, till the eruption of the flood of revolution and war would effect great destruction of life and property. But also in the case, that the enemies of the old institutions would succeed so far as to sweep away every vestige of them on the surface of the Globe, they would be as little able as the supporters of the old systems to preserve Peace; because there is no pacification in the spirit world, except by receiving and spreading the means shown us from the spheres of spirits by whom we are commissioned to introduce the New Era of Harmony and Peace amongst mortals as well as amongst their congenial departed. But the more materialism subdues the Globe, the more the inner causes for new out-breaks of revolutions and wars are operating to find crevices for the outbreak, so that there is absolutism and despotism as necessary for those who without the use of the old forms promise to make people free, as for those who promise the same in the support of the new systems. Emperor Louis Napoleon and Emperor Francis Joseph are quite remarkable representatives of the two systems, while Napoleon makes such a use of the old form as to satisfy many of the open opposers to it, and the Emperor of Austria endeavours to sustain with hundreds of thousands of soldiers the inheritance of the old abominations which should have been abolished by the application of our message without murder of any man and for the greatest benefit of the departed and the mortals of the family of Hapsburgh, while the whole empire and all nations would have been benefited.

From the scattered hints in this book you may collect, that since Francis Joseph's Government I was rather endeavouring to effect in one or the other manner a movement in this country, by which at length also the Bishops and the Government of Austria might be awakened from their fatal lethargy; because I saw that my direct applications to the young Emperor would have been for no use. I am in no direct correspondence with my native country, and I receive news either in newspapers or from occasional reports, and shortly before I wrote the weighty Epistle to Anthony Slomshek I met with a countryman who was professor in Vienna, during the revolution of 1848, and on account that he inspired students for fighting, he had to leave the country, and he told me besides other news, that he heard that Anthony Slomshek was Prince Bishop in Laibach. Several years before that I received the news that he was Prince Bishop at Saint Andrew in Lavant Valley of Carinthia, only five miles from the monastery of Saint Paul, where I became a monk of the Benedictine order. I wrote to him, when I received that report; but I received no answer. At length the Epistle which appears in this treatise, has been sent to him as to Prince Bishop of Laibach, on the above mentioned authority. The Epistle would retain in this book the same value also in the case, that the report should not be correct that he is Bishop of Laibach; because the facts which I relate in the Epistle as facts known to him are facts of my own experience and such as occurred in close connection with my experience, and have been attested by many witnesses directly after they happened.

Although I made few applications directly to Austria during the Government of Emperor Francis Joseph, my fellow student Frederick Baraga, Bishop at the Falls of Saint Mary at Lake Superior, extending his diocese widely amongst Indians of North America, a peculiar favorite at the Austrian Court, after having neglected the former opportunities to study our message of Peace and to spread it in the Austrian Government, was brought on the great Popish Feast of Christ's Body (Festum Corporis Christi) May 22, 1856, to me in quite an unexpected manner for both but in such a connexion with the present war in Europe, that if this man, at least at that time had fulfilled his highest duty, instead of the tremendous war, Christ's Peace would have already been established in Europe. Therefore, not having room to write much, I must mention at least somewhat about that our meeting showing the secret causes of the present war and of all revolutions and wars since our first proclamation of the great message entrusted to our care.

On that feast, which was celebrated A. D. 1856 on the 22d day of May, my pamphlet: "Redemption of oppressed Humanity! Christ's manifestation for the abolition of all kinds of Popery!" issued from the press in the same Printing Establishment of Cincinnati, into which Bishop Baraga came on that feast to see the proof-sheet of the title page of his Latin Book for his missionaries. Our meeting on that feast in a Protestant Printing Office was so unexpected, that we did not know each other, when we met at the compositors' room which he left while I was entering into it. I was then instructed by the compositors, that that gentleman was the same Bishop Baraga about whom I spoke in the pamphlet showing that while bishops were consecrating him or made him a bishop, they were crucifying Christ in his members; to wit, that bishop after having become so great an apostle of the Indians, that he was very renowned in our native country and at the Austrian

Government, was made a medium by my leaders, that he opened the way for my voyage to America. But after having discovered, that our mission was not for, but against the Pope, he instead of having studied my books and examined our message of Peace and the credentials of onr mission, became enraged. I expected that at a personal meeting with him I would make him comprehend our mission. But there was no opportunity until that feast on the 22d May, 1856, which was selected for the commencement of the spirit manifestations at my personal meetings with that medium of spirits of delusion and destruction.

After having written a considerable portion of the next following treatise, I am aware that I cannot encompass within so few pages as I am desirous to do, what is to be communicated there to nations, and I take from this treatise some sheets away, in which I have given disclosures, why we have mentioned in our Epistle to Bishop Anthony Slomshek also the Bishops of Triest and Goricia, whose predecessors should have at the same time opened the way to the circulation of our message of Peace in which time Bishop Anthony Aloysy Wolf should have been their cooperator for Peace. But Matthew Raunicher, who was at that time Bishop of Triest, should have been the leader of this work; because amongst those who belonged to the Austrian Government he was the first who received the first two volumes of my works. But he was formerly Professor of Dogmatics and as such also my professor, and was so fixed in the Dogmas of his infallible Church, that he could not study my books, to learn what all dogmatists of the so called christian denominations require, to with signs according to prophecies by which an "extraordinary ambassador" to the churches should prove his mission. I hope, that Raunicher's disciples, Bishop Baraga and Bishops and Priests in Illyria and elsewhere will learn at length that we have superabundance of signs according to prophecies testifying our mission against the infallibility of the Church, and for the great truth, that many of the Dogmas of the church are the most shocking absurdities, of they are taken as they have been delivered by the

Papal Imperial Royal Hierarchy, but that we show a deeper sense, in which sound reason and science are reconciled with religion. But we close this treatise to get more room for the next following treatise, to assist the Pope and his bishops to prepare for their own and the ressurrection of their departed predecessors.

FOURTH TREATISE.

Pious IX Bishop of Rome, Louis Napoleon Emperor of France, Francis Joseph Emperor of Austria, the three extraordinary witnesses of our on the title-page of this book expressed mission and powerful preachers to all governments and in the first place to the Government of the United States of North America, that they should submit to the Government of our Lord and his Christ and become with us messengers to introduce the promised universal Republic of Truth and Justice, Harmony and Peace on the whole Globe.

In the first three of my five German volumes the magnetic chain of memorable events to bind the dragon, Revel xx: 2, is so developed, that the proper position of the existing governments of the so called christians is mademanifest. They belong to the Beast with seven heads and to its ten horns either in the old or in a new fashion. Those three volumes having been published from A. D. 1838 to 1840, Pope Pius IX and the two named Emperors towhom the world's attention is now directed, have not been mentioned in those volumes nor known to mortal men, that they will occupy the position, on which they appear according to prophecies, nor they themselves nor other men know at this time that position, if they have not studied the magnetic chain exhibited in those volumes to bind the dragon, Revel. xx.: 2, the large serpent, the image of the spirit of delusion and destruction by whom rulers and their supporters have been inspired with such a madness as to apply their studies how to kill men in the most cunning manner and to strip the remnant of their property and keep them in bondage. Each of those volumes is of a considerable size; the third is the largest containing 864 pages. But the substance of their contents is concentrated in the Latin manuscript, written at the commencement of 1849.

If Theologians had studied my German volumes or attended the Latin Convention to which they have been most earnestly invited, they had known without my explanation the position of these three great representatives, or rather they had converted them long ago into the messengers of Peace. But after matters had arrived so far as they are now manifest, we must do what we can for the benefit of these three witnesses and of those who are attached to one or the other as well as for the benefit of all governments and their subjects; because all are preparing instruments for destruction of human life and property and drilling men to destroy or wound their fellow men in the most artful and cunning manner, and to reward with the highest premiums those who perform best this most criminal work.

If you ask, by whose authority they are doing this, the answer is given: "and the Dragon gave him his power, and his seat and great authority," Revel. XIII: 2. to wit, to the representative of the Beast with seven heads and ten horns. Under the christian mask he became such a terrible monster, that no other epithet was more suitable for him than that of a Therion, of a ferocious beast having seven heads and ten horns. Having been inspired and directed by the Dragon and his host, he could not teach his sons and daughters, emperors and empresses, kings and queens, a better doctrine than that which was infixed in his heads by the Dragon and his host. "The seven heads are seven mountains, on which the woman sitteth; and they are seven kings; five are fallen, and one is, and the other is not yet come; and when he comes, he must continue a short space." Revel xvii: 9 and 10.

It is to be understood, that in a brief treatise we can give only some hints in regard to certain links of the long chain of events, which is exhibited in the first three from A. D. 1838 to 1840 published volumes. The three at the head of this treatise mentioned witnesses are so extraordinary links added to that chain, that while I was writing those three volumes I thought, that the chain was long and strong enought to bind the Dragon and to establish Peace on the whole Globe. But when people would not spread that chain, it was after that much protracted. In the years 1841 and 1842 the 4th and 5th German volumes and then a number of English pamphlets were added; but the last links of the chain cannot be understood without some knowledge of the preceding links.

In every age men were awakened, whose intellectual and moral improvement was above the general course of the age, and who were endeavoring to warn and elevate the fallen generation. They were preparing the way for our advent, and disclosing what belonged to their sphere, that it might receive more light in "the dispensation of the fulness of times" Ephes. 1 : 10, to introduce which we are commissioned. One of those forerunners was Doctor Bengel, disclosing what belonged to his mission in the first half of the last century, so that in the same years of the 18th century remarkable disclosures have been made by his instrumentality, in which years in the 19th century Heavenly messengers have given great disclosures by my instrumentality regarding Christ's peaceable reign on earth. A. D. 1740 his German work "Erklaerte Offenbarung (Revelation explained) was published; and exactly one hundred years after that, on Easter Saturday, 1840, my third German volume, by which the chain to bind the Dragon was complete, issued from the press. To wit, in the first and second volumes the "memorable events" are reported, which took place at our experience for the abolition of Popery, or what is the same, for the abolition of monarchy ; and in the third volume is shown, that memorable events which are explained in my first two volumes, happened according to prophecies which are in the Bible and also in other works of ancient times and have been repeated through the course of centuries of the Christian Era, and that the memorable events which happened at our experience, would not have scared priests and preachers, but would have been expected by them, if they had not been ignoramuses of what our forerunners had disclosed before us, or stubborn materialistic hypocrites, not beleaving what they preach and profess by their performance.

The principal of those forerunners have been mentioned in that volume, and how far each in his situation saw the objects, which have received in our mission a light which could not be obtained in former ages. Doctor Bengel occupies amongst those forerunners a peculiar place ; because he is the second angel or messenger, spoken of in Revel. xiv: 8, that is, the representative of messengers by whom the contents of that verse are fulfilled, because he was the first amongst those, who have proclaimed prophetically Christ's coming or Christ's manifestation to effect the fall of Babylon while they were showing the time in which it had to take place, and disclosing many other deep things which were not known before, and have warned people powerfully, to prepare for Christ's coming. This was done by Doctor Bengel and his disciples prophetically, I mean, that they saw Christ's coming only in the image of the Biblical prophets, and did not know the manner of his coming, and pointed out the year **1836**, as the tropical year for his coming. But when that year expired, those who had before great confidence in Dr. Bengel's disclosures, said, that he was mistaken in the calculation of the times. But we have shown according to our mission in the 3rd. of the mentioned volumes, that Doctor Bengel was not mistaken in what belonged to the sphere of his mission, and his wonderful calculation was correct regarding the time, but that what he wrote regarding the manner of Christ's coming and other things were not correct, which not he but the third angel, Revel. xiv. 8, had to disclose; because the year 1836 was the tropical year, at the expiration of which the 3d angel had to appear, and then to perform his task and explain the prophetical images and other things which have not been understood before that explanation; because the Lord came at that time as a thief, Revel. xvi : 15. The thief is not seen, when he takes away what he finds suitable for his use And the same have we done in our mission in which was gradually disclosed, that Christ comes by us, his messengers, and discloses what is needed, by the direction of his invisible agents who are operating through our mediumship.

If you keep all that has been said in this book, you will comprehend the hints which we have given as preparations at our approach to the development of what we have promised in the inscription of this treatise. Others have tried to show from their position, and Doctor Bengel with application of historical and astronomical erudition endeavoured to make it most evident, that the Beast with seven heads and ten horns in the 13th chapter of the Revelation, is the papal monarchy. At length came the 3rd angel or messenger, Revel. xiv : 9, by whose mediumship the whole chain was developed, which testifies the same. And Heavenly Congress of the 144,000 martyrs, Revel. xiv : 1, who superintend, that prophecy given under their direction, is exactly fulfilled, (as there is the case with the prophecies of the Revelation,) have given also such testimonies of this truth, that the most stubborn materialist if he studies to learn truth, finds superabundance of most striking evidences, that hosts of spirits were co-operating, that prophecy was fulfilling, till at length by unexpected events the Divine seal was attached to its fulfilment by our mediumship. We will give later in this treatise striking testimonies of this truth. But here was the preparation, that you may understand the following hints on the 9th and 10th verses of the 17th chapter of the Revelation in connection with the inscription of this treatise.

Doctor Bengel was the first who has discovered, after an investigation for many years in the Bullarium Romanum, in which the dates of the papal letters which are known under the name of the Papal Bulls, bear besides the time, the place from which they issued, that is, the place of the Papal See or Chair, or of the papal government. In the 17th chapter is the same Beast with the seven heads and ten horns which appears in the first verse of the 13th chapter, only that in the 17th chapter it appears in another state, to wit, the seer says in Revelation, xvii : 3d, I saw a woman sit upon a scarlet coloured beast, full of names of blasphemy, having seven heads and ten horns." This woman is called in the 5th verse : "Babylon the great, the mother of harlots and abominations." The same woman is called in the 3d verse of the second chapter in the second epistle to the Thessalonians "the apostasia or apostasy," what your translators expressed with "a falling away." In the preceding treatise we quoted a prophecy in the 33d song of Purgatory in Dante's Divine comedy, in which the five hundred ten and five messenger of God strangles the harlot and the giant who sins with the harlot. That harlot is the same old woman, which is called in the 17th chapter of the Revelation, "the mother of harlots and abominations," and the giant is the representative of the Beast, at this time Pius ix, carrying on his shoulders the whole burden of abominations and blasphemies of the whole succession of the apostles whose master is the apocalyptical dragon, who has given him "power, seat and great authority," Revel. xiii : 2. The word which is in your translation seat, is in Greek "throne," which you understand. But by the worshipers of the Beast it is usually called "the Holy See," and you know if you have comprehended this book until this page, that the Pope had received his holy see from "his infernal holiness, the dragon." And we will concentrate and kindle an admireable light upon this subject in this treatise.

In the the 7th chapter of Daniel is the 4th Beast, having ten horns, the Roman Monarchy. This same monarchy became at length the papal monarchy, when the Bishop of Rome became monarch of the chnrch and extended his monarchy or superintendency over the other monarchs and nations as far as he could, with the same view, as the heathen Roman Emperors had, to make Rome the mistress of the globe ; only that the Roman bishop did this under a christian title, although his government was an antichristian government under a christian pretext. There was inspiration ; but the inspiration was from the dragon and his host. The foundation of that Empire is expressed in Revel. xiii : 2. Any body who has a christian spirit and compares that which happened in Italy from Easter Sunday of this year until this day, July, 21st, 1859, is convinced of this truth. These are the fruits of the Papal monarchy ! I have superabundance of other business, and am writing occasionally since the 4th of this month the preceding and this treatise, and the reader should keep continuously in his mind, that I give only some links in this time of great delusion preparing great destruction also in this country, that there not being opportunity to study the whole chain of our disclosures people might receive as much as necessary to know the " secret ememies of true Republicanism," and the inner life of man and the spirit world, that they might be saved, instead of being ruined and destroyed. "The seven heads are seven mountains. Also seven kings, five of whom are fallen, and one is and the other is not yet come." This is the state of things at the time, in the 9th and 10th verses of the 17th chapter of the Revelation. Rome is located on a number of hills, the seven principal of which are called by the ancient writers the seven mountains. Doctor Bengel has shown from the Bullarium Romanum and other documents regarding the Papal government, that since the Roman Emperor Constantine I. the Pope had the seat of his administration until the time in which Doctor Bengel wrote, on five of the seven mountains, to wit, 1. on the mountain Coelius, 2. mountain Aventinus, 3. Vaticanus, 4. Qurinalis, 5. Esquilinus. Farther is to be remarked that although Popes had some times their seatsin other places, for instance in Avignon of France, others in opposition to them had at the same time their seat in Rome, or when in some Revolution they were driven from Rome, they returned as soon as they could. Doctor Bengel when he found, that in his time the seat of the Papal government was the fifth of the seven mountains, assured most solemnly, that that government would not be translocated from that upon another mountain until it crumbled to pieces, and he, by his admirable calculation, showed, that it would take place before the expiration of his century. It took place A. D. 1798, when Pope Pius VI. was taken captive and carried to France, and the French Directory located the seat of their government in Rome, not upon one of the five mountains which were successively occupied as the seat of the Papal government, but upon the mountain Capitolinus. On that mountain was the temple which was dedicated during the heathen Rome to all heathen Gods, and during the Papal Rome to all Saints or all Gods whom the Pope professed to worship. But then it was taken by the French Directory for the seat of the government.

All these things were axactly performed by the influence of spirits of different spheres. Every actor in the great drama was influenced by spirits for whose inspiration he was best prepared. But all that took place under the vigilance of the highest order of spirits for the accomplishment of prophecies. In Revelation, xvii : 10 the seven mountains are called seven kings, that is seven monarchial or despotic or antichristian governments, governments which originated from the inspiration of the dragon, the spirit of delusion and destruction. The seven mountains are types of these seven governments. But five are fallen, that is five kings or five monarchial governments are fallen at the time which the Revelator saw, that is, at the time, when the woman was sitting on the Beast having seven heads and ten horns. During those five kings or during the Papal governments on the five mountains that woman, which is the mother of harlots and abominations, was prepared and fostered by all the anti-christian deeds which have been perpetrated by the authority of the Papal Bulls which issued from the five mountains. People who came out from the exterior fashion of Popery, did not return to the christian truth and christian spirit, but progressed into materialism and endeavoured to effect with weapons of war, what can only be effected according to the plan given in the following treatise. The French Revolution broke out A. D. 1789, and progressed in tremendous destruction of life and property and in terrorism and distress of the survivors, that at length A. D. 1798 Pope Pious VI was carried captive to France, where he died ; the Papal Monarchy or the Beast having seven heads, disappeared, or the woman was sitting upon the Beast, that is, took possession of the monarchy. That woman is called the harlot and the mother of harlots, and the apostasy, or defection from truth and righteousness. People polluted with this defection appear under the image of a harlot. And those who professed to act in the name of the Republic or the people, after having removed the Pope from his seat, located their government on the Mountain Capitolinus, in contempt of the saints or gods of the Pope, and supported their government with a more terrible despotism, than their predecessors, the popes, did. This government of the French Directory on the Mountain Capitolinus, is in this calculation the sixth government, or the government introduced in Rome after the fall of the governments on the five of the seven mountains. When the government on those five mountains was translocated from one mountain upon an other, the government was not destroyed but only changed, as circumstances required. But when the sixth government, (called in Revel. xvii 10: "the one is" that is, the one which was in existence after the fall of the preceding five), was introduced, the former governments of the Papal monarchy were entirely abolished. When this took place, "the other" in Revel. xvii: 10 "was not yet come," and the government of the French Republic was in the greatest danger of being overturned. In those circumstances, "the other," that is Napoleon came. He returned from Egypt and saved the republic; but the republic could not be sustained, and Napoleon advanced gradually so far that he became at length Emperor; and of him is said: "he must continue a short space." Revel xvii: 10. His government is in this calculation the seventh government. He thought, that the secular monarchy of the Pope was injurious to his Empire, and he required that the Pope, Pious VII, successor of Pius VI who died in France, should give up his secular monarchy. And when the Pope refused to do so, he was taken captive and brought at length to France.

Napoleon is in our magnetic chain the same, who according to the vulgar reading and translation is called "the man of sin, the son of perdition." 2d Ep. Thessal. ii: 3. We give only as many hints as are sufficient, to arouse governments and nations from their lethargy. Theologians not knowing how the Bible originated, nor how to make the right use of it, had made already of the first chapter of the Bible the greatest abuse, and came in collision with developments of astronomy and geology as well as with the true history of man, being in that chapter nothing else but the vision or the image of the creation of the mosaic Heaven and the mosaic Earth, or the mosaic ecclesiastical and political institutions, which are abolished by virtue of our mission in which we show the new Heaven and the new Earth. Interpretors and translators commenced to dupe people with the first verse of the Bible, where the Hebrew word "Elohim" is in the plural number But they translated that word, "God;" although those who know somewhat about the true spiritualism, may easily comprehend, that those Elohim are the guardian gods or the guardian angels, departed ancestors of the Jewish Nation. At the administration of those guardians Moses produced the ecclesiastical and political institutions of that nation. Of those institutions. and of the books of that nation such a tremendous abuse was made, that from that abuse at length "the man of sin, the son of perdition" was produced. But this vulgar reading is taken in the first place from a wrong Greek reading. The genuine reading gives in the first place the translation "the man of lawlessness" that is, the man who came out from a lawless state, from a state in which the ecclesiastical and political laws have been overthrown. In the second place instead of "the son of perdition" should be translated "the son of destruction," that is, the man who came through that dreadful destruction of human life and property which is preserved in history, upon the Imperial Throne of France, that all in him has been fulfilled, what we read in the quoted chapter, and is explained in our magnetic chain in which we have given also the genuine reading and the genuine translation, where needed to understand the prophecy, as far as it has been fulfiilled in Napoleon I. But the explanation cannot be here repeated; but we had here to mention as much as necessary, that the supplement of its fulfilment might be understood by Napoleon III. and that the two fighting emperors and their tremendous armies in Italy, as well as all other monarchs, might learn their true position and be converted from the Dragon to Christ and become with us messengers of Peace. For this purpose we must give the following hints:

"And the Beast that was and is not, even he is the eighth, and is of the seven, and goeth into perdition. Revel. xvii.: 11. You must keep in mind, that the Revelator saw the state in which the harlot was sitting on the Beast, that is, occupying the place of the Papal monarchy, In that state of things the Beast or Papal monarchy was not in existence. But when the Revelator was contemplating that state with marvel, the angel who has shown him this state of things, gives some prophecies of what would follow after that state.

"The Beast that thou sawest, was, and is not; and shall ascend out of the bottomless pit, and go into perdition" Revel. xvii; 8. The Papal monarchy, which disappeared for a certain time, had to re-appear, and that re-appearance is its ascension from the abyss, from so deep a cave that its bottom is not seen, from the realm of darkness in reference to Revel. xiii: 2, when it came into existence first by the spirit of delusion effecting great destruction, at the incursion of babarian nations into the Roman Empire in the 4th, 5th, and 6th centuries. At that time the Bishop of Rome took advantage to commence to be Superintendent of the kingdoms which originated from the Roman Empire, and their number was successively ten, which are called the ten horns of the Beast. Napoleon's Empire "which continued a short space," having been the seventh government, the Papal monarchy which ascended out of the abyss Revel. xvii: 8, was in this calculation the eighth king or government, Revel. xvii: 11, and came out of the seven preceding governments, and commenced, when A. D. 1814 Pope Pius VII took possession of his territory after his triumphant return to Rome. Then the ten horns of the Beast, who "are ten kings" Revel. xvii: 12, (to wit, in reference to the origin of the kingdoms out of the Roman Empire in connexion with the origin of the papal monarchy,) the monarchs or their Representatives who after the overthrow of Napoleon's Empire assembled in the Congress of Vienna, "These have one mind, and shall give their power and strength unto the Beast." Revel. xvii: 13 The translation being not exact, we give only the sense, that they agreed, that the representative of the Beast or the Pope should be with them a partaker of his temporal power, or of his monarchy, which he has lost entirely during the sixth government, and died in captivity. His successor Pius VII, who commenced to restore it, was then taken by Napoleon; but after Napoleon's fall the old dynasties with the Papal monarchy were restored. And the people continued in the great apostasy which is called the harlot, and the monarchs were fulfilling and continue to fulfil at this time in the most tremendous manner the 16th verse of the 17th chapter of the Revelation, "making the harlot desolate and naked, eating her flesh and burning her with fire." In this tremendous condition they continued since they took again possession of their governments. Their proceedings and the whole management of their affairs appear anti-christian. These governments "make war with the lamb." Revel. xvii : 14. This they do continously, till at length we read reports of such destructions as are now in Italy. But to those who are with the lamb, called and chosen and faithful, the victory against the antichristian governments is promised in the same verse. Without having room for farther hints in this confinement to a small book, that it might be studied by many who could not be moved or would not have time to study a large work or would not have the means to buy it, we must give here some hints, how our victory against those who are in war with the lamb, has been secured by the most solemn promises and fulfilment of the most sublime prophecies. Readers should keep in mind all hints given on the preceding pages, and should know, that I was called to America by a Heavenly messenger. Then followed continuous signs, by which all things were prepared the right moment, that I was directed to Boston, Mass., and arrived in that city on my birth day, November, 29, 1837, when I was exactly 42 years old. I had no knowledge, that my invisible guardians had prepared all that was required, that in that city great works have been performed by my instrumentality. On memorable events which happened in the Roman Catholic Church of that city from December, 1837, until the 3d Sunday after Easter, 1838, by my mediumship and assistance of 144 witnesses many hundred pages have been written in my often mentioned five German volumes.

Readers of this book are accustomed to hear unexpected events, and we mention without explanations the following as preparatory to the light which we shall give in this treatise upon the present meeting of Emperor Napoleon and his army with Emperor Francis Joseph and his army in Italy, and upon the present Pope in their vicinity.

While I was preparing to start from Boston to other places, I was instructed by unexpected wonders and signs that I must remain in Boston and take care of the German Catholic congregation, and the priest who had charge of it, was by invisible agents compelled to leave directly Boston. For the use of our German Congregation the Roman Catholic Cathedral Church was granted at the time, during which it was not occupied by the Irish and American Congregation. We had our service on sundays from 8 to 10 o'clock A. M. in that Church, and I explained prophecies in reference to our time and the necessity of true Reformation for those who would be partakers of the great promises for the fulfilment of which the time was approaching. This I knew as well as also, that I came to America to work in this country for their fulfilment according to the direction of my leaders. But I did not know, what, according to their plan was to be done.

On the 6th day of January, 1838, which was Saturday and the feast of Epiphany or Christ's manifestation, a great prophetical feast for our mission, I received the order from my guardian, the martyr in Revel. xiv : 14, who was crucified and burned by the Pope, and found by the Heavenly Congress, Revel. xiv : 1, as best qualified to be my principal director in what I had to perform in the cathedral Church in Boston. The name of that martyr and why he was found to be my leader in that work, is in other of my writings. By him I was instructed to prepare the congregation on that feast, that those who would be willing to cooperate with us for the great Reformation which was required for the fulfilment of prophecies, should be ready to come on the next following day after our Sunday service in my school room and sign their names and what they would be willing to do for defraying expenses in our enterprises. On sunday the 7th of January, 1838, I delivered again a sermon suitable to inspire the congregation for the great enterprise, and asked that those who were ready for co-operation, should come directly after the service in our school room. That was a step against all precedence. The catalogue of those who belonged to the congregation, was given to me before, and trustees took great care to collect large subscriptions for us. But all this should be rejected, and only those who would be ready to work with me for the great reformation without regard to the bishop, should come and sign their names and contributions, to be regarded as my fellow labourers in the great reformation. Although I have explained to them in my sermons as many signs as they could bear, that I came against all my expectations to America to prepare people for the reformation necessary for the fulfilment of the greatest promises, I, according to human insight into matters, did not expect that any would dare to sign his name. But I did, as I was ordered by my leader.

After our service on Sunday, January 7, 1859, there came so many that our school room was crowded. Trustees and others came with them to warn the others, not to do any step for such an enterprise, without asking first the bishop, what should be done in this case. Others remarked, that I knew well what I was doing. And I repeated what I have explained at our meetings in the church, that I was doing nothing except what was showed to me by the spirit, who had given also in their presence sufficient testimonies, that he was a spirit of truth and righteousness. Then all were so inspired, that those who resisted most signed first their names. Having been agreed that they must sign their names before me and witnesses in my catalogue the business required time, and those who came from a distance, remained to sign their names amongst the first, and the others went home, and returned afternoon. On the next following Sunday we assembled again, that the names of the signers were read solemnly and distinctly in the presence of the whole congregation for other purposes, which to mention here is no room, as well as for the purpose which must be mentioned, that the congregation were expressly admonished, that at the reading of the names of the signers they should pay pecular attention, that if any mistake should be found, it might be corrected, and that all might be witnesses of what every one had signed to contribute for our enterprise. Every one, called by the name, answered. Most of them, if not all, were present. And if any one, for I do not recollect any case, was absent, certainly those who knew him and were present when he came to sign his name, testified, that they saw him, when he signed his name and contribution, and that his name was correctly written into my catalogue. In this manner that which was signed January 7th 1838, before witnesses was on the 14th of the same month testified by the whole congregation.

Signs and wonders became more manifest. I was commanded by my leader to write an Encyclic Latin Epistle, directed to the Bishops of the Austrian Empire, showing the necessity of true Reformation that nations might become partakers of the promises. I have shown in that Epistle of seven closely written sheets, what was first and most necessary; and I mentioned a number of signs which have been given in the Austrian Empire before I started thence to America, and a number of signs in Boston after my arrival there, by which our mission was testified. After having finished writing that Epistle, I was directed by the same spirit, to write to Benedict Fenwick Roman Catholic Bishop of Boston, a short letter, as addition to the Encyclic Epistle to the Bishops of Austria, showing to the bishops, that whereas some signs have been mentioned, which took place in the Austrian Empire in the presence of witnesses who have been named in the Epistle, and other signs happened in Boston, and of those signs he was a witness, he was in duty bound to sign first the circular Epistle and to promise his co-operation with us for the great Reformation of the Church, which is necessary to stop judgments and to make nations partakers of the greatest promises. I added, that if he would refuse to sign, I could not go any more into his Church. The bishop was a cunning Jesuite. He understood that by signing that Epistle he could not satisfy his Pope, and he wrote to me a very enticing letter, to stop me in my Reformation. But I assembled directly those of the congregation, who could be assembled that evening, Friday, February 16th, 1838, and explained what had happened, showing to them their duty, to make known to the congregation to assemble on next Sunday in a Protestant School-house in which I would explain, why I could not go any more into the Church of the Bishop. I convinced them after sufficient explanation of the matter, that they were satisfied, that I had to obey rather the direction of the spirit, than the wishes of the bishop.

On Saturday, Feb. 17, 1838, I was again awakened at 3 o'clock A. M. as at my former commission, and commanded by my leader, to write again to the bishop and explain my message given to the congregation to assemble on the next day in a Protestant School house unless the bishop would acknowledge his fault and do what was required. I assured him most solemnly, that all those steps were done under strict direction of the spirit who had confirmed my mission; therefore "nisi haec feceris, tecum in sacris communicare non possum." It is to be understood, that I wrote to him in Latin, and said: "If thou, Bishop, wilt not do this," that is, if thou wilt not sign the Epistle and co-operate with us, "I can have no ecclesiastical communion with thee." The Epistle was then carried and handed to him at 8 o'clock A. M. of that day.

Soon after that a deputation of our congregation came to me. They reported that our message according to our agreement, was spread in the congregation, but there was a means, to satisfy the spirit; because the Catholic Cathedral Church does not belong to the bishop, but to the nations. The deputation assured me that Roman Catholics and Protestants of different nations have contributed freely to build that church, and I could explain freely in the church what I had to communicate to the congregation; since neither the bishop nor any of his priests understood German. It was evident, that one of the three was under the influence of a prudent spirit. But I replied, that in steps of such consequence I must act strictly according to the order of the spirit. They should therefore go to the bishop. Perhaps they might move him to sign the Epistle. They went; but they returned with the message, that they found the bishop not well, entreating me very much that although he could not sign my encyclic Epistle, I should go in the church, and difficulties would be then amicably settled. From that circumstance I understood, that the bishop did not comprehend what it was, to receive a commission by Heavenly messengers, which was sufficiently attested as sent from Heaven. Therefore I said to the committee, that after the bishop had remained in such a darkness, I must strictly act according to the direction of the spirit who has sent me. Then the man who was under influence was stronger moved to urge me to go in the church, without regard to the bishop, and explain what I wished to communicate to the congregation. When the other two belonging to the committee thought that I could not be moved, they left my room. Then the third was stronger moved by his leader than before, to urge me to go in the church. Then my leader brought to me the distinct message, that I should go into the church and perform independently from all bishops, what would be shown to me to be performed. At that unexpected message I said to the man, that I have received the communication which I needed to tell to the congregation, that they should assemble on the next day in the church.

From the message I understood, that after having excommunicated the bishop from my ecclesiastical communion, and in my last letter more distinctly than in my first, I had to omit in my performances in the church all that shows any communication with the bishop or with the Pope, whose representative the bishop was. But I knew long before that, that the Roman Catholic Church was a prophetical church, and I had to perform the prophetical ceremonies which were in use at those days on which I had to go in the church. The prophetical spirit has so provided for what I had to perform from that moment in the church, that at every performance also the passages which were taken from the Bible into the Roman Catholic mass-book and ritual, corresponded exactly with what I was doing.

On the 18th February, 1838, which was Sunday Sexagesima, I came the first time independently from all bishops, into the Roman Catholic Cathedral Church of Boston, Mass. to do what would be shown to me by inspiration. The church has prepared for that Sunday from the 11th and 12th chapters of the 2d Epistle to Corinthians the sufferings of the Apostle Paul and his report, that he was caught up to the third Heaven. When I was reading at the Altar that section, and came to the quoted passage, "I was caught up to Heaven." Paul the Prophet, as he appears in our mission, did not know, whether it was in or out of his body. But I know I was entranced, while my body was immoveable at the Altar, and Heavenly power was communicated to me, and I was ordered to explain to the audience the testimonies of my mission, commencing with the initiation which I have received twelve years before that. To wit, A. D. 1825 after my having been six years secular Priest, testimonies were given, that I was called to join with Priests of the Benedictine Order. I felt that there were sufficient testimonies of my call from Heaven. But after my having moved into the monastery, matters appeared so contrary to my expectation, that I thought, that my surest way would be to write to the next bishop and to continue to labor as secular Priest. In that my determination to write on the next following day to the Bishop of Lavant, I went to rest. But I came from my sleep into a trance of unspeakable Heavenly light, during which I was surrounded by a company of spirits and magnetized or initiated by them for the great labor which I had to perform, and the temptations against which I had to act. At that initiation I did not see my mother, but I heard so distinctly her voice and with so powerful impression that it could not be effaced from my mind, when she said that I should remain in the monastery. Amongst all communications which I received in Europe from Heavenly guides, this was the only one, which I have received from my mother; and nobody else could impress a stronger conviction than she did, in the most momentous instance in which I needed a Heavenly comfort. And that initiation by Heavenly messengers strengthened me, till I received on Sunday Sexagesima, February 18, 1838, the great initiation at the Altar of the Cathedral Church of Boston for my public appearance in my present charge and was commanded by the martyr Revel. xiv: 14 to commence my address with the initiation which I had received twelve years before that. The Roman Catholic Church has prepared for that Sunday Luke viii 4-15, and I explained according to the 10th verse the mystery of our mission. I had to mention some points at my public initiation to my present mission in which I had to perform in the first place in the Roman Catholic Church what was required according to prophecies to give the Pope and his bishops the most solemn divine testimony, that their prophetical administration is accomplished, and that their highest duty is to become with us messengers of the dispensation of the fulness of times Ephes. 1: 10, in which all in Heaven and on Earth should be united and pacified in Christ. For this purpose the church or the people must be cleansed. To show them the necessity of the cleansing of the sanctuary, after that my public appearance in the glorious mission, demons were compelled to bring to daylight the secret abominations, of which we have in the brief hints of this treatise to mention one instance, which is in peculiar connexion with the three on the title-page named witnesses and with other regents. One man was found in our congregation, who was not in the catalogue of the 144, who have signed their names into our catalogue on the 7th January, 1838; but he was in the catalogue of those who have been given to me before that signing as belonging to the congregation, and that man appeared in that catalogue as being married, and when after our public appearance in the present mission the abominations commenced to be detected, that man was found, that he was not married with the woman with whom he lived as being married. I sent to him word, that if he wished to know his duty, he should come to me. But he would not come. This happened in the week after my public appearance in my present charge. I asked, whether the case was known in the congregation, and I was told, that it was known. On the next following Sunday, which was Quinquagesima or the next Sunday before Lent, I received the order from my leader to excommunicate that man publicly. I delivered a sermon appropriate to the case, mentioned that such a man was in the congregation, without naming him, and made the declaration that such a man does not belong to the church of Christ or to our congregation till he is converted from his illegal connection.

After that many other performances of our mission took place, which cannot be mentioned here, except the following:

According to the agreement the signers of their names and contributions for our support and to defray the necessary expenses, had to bring a portion of their contribution before Palm Sunday 1838' which is the Sunday before Easter, and if somebody should be hindered in doing what he agreed to do, he should come and mention his reason, or if he could not come himself, he should send word by some other. In the case, that he would neglect to do the one or the other, we would send, to inquire for the reason of his having neglected his duty. This was to be mentioned for the right comprehension of the unexpected events which we must in this connexion of things report as briefly as possible.

In the night from Palm Sunday to Monday I was at one o'clock by a shock suddenly awakened and I heard the voice: "Arise and take from the catalogue those who had neither brought their contributions, nor the excuse why they could not do so, and excommunicate them on the next Sunday solemnly from Christ's Church." I arose directly, made light, took them from my catalogue and put them on another paper. Then I became suddenly very drowsy and returned to bed. When I arose at the usual time, I reflected upon the unexpected communication, and I thought, that my duty was to inquire for the men, and that only under the condition that they would obstinately resist to submit to the rules of our order, they would deserve a public declaration, that they do not belong to Christ's Church. Also it appeared quite strange, that Easter Sunday was appointed for that excommunication. I thought, that if I would send for and converse with them, I would perhaps find out the reason of such an unexpected order. Besides all other things I had also the most convenient lodging for my performances in the new mission. But here we select only those points which are preparatory to the development of deep secrets by which the three extraordinary men mentioned on the title-page become extraordinary witnesses of our mission. The merchant with whom I boarded knew most persons of our congregation. Therefore I took the paper on which I put the names according to the Heavenly commission, and asked him whether he knew any of those persons who were on the paper. After his negative answer I called our messenger to give him the paper with the order to inquire at those who were acquainted with most people of our congregation, to find out those persons and invite them to come to me about important matters, without telling the case which I myself did not understand. But at the moment, when I would give him the paper, I was severly shaken and heard the voice, not to inquire for any body but to perform that which I had been commanded to do.

The order having been given by the leader from whom other most important orders came, I was satisfied, that with the order were deeper things connected than I could expect. I asked the messenger whether he heard any voice. He replied in the negative. I understood that I was taken by him into the inner state, when he shook me and said to me not to inquire for anybody, but to perform the order.

From Monday to Tuesday in the week before Easter I was again shaken and awakened by my leader at 1 o'clock A. M. and heard his voice: "Arise and write for the book the order given on the preceding night to be executed on next Sunday. To understand this order I must remark, that soon after my declaration made to Bishop Fenwick of Boston, that if he refuses to sign the Epistle I can have no ecclesiastical communion with him, which declaration was a polite manner in which I excommunicated the bishop, I commenced to write a book, showing that my extraordinary steps were made under higher direction testifying my extraordinary mission; because as soon as I was ordered to separate from the bishop, and to perform independently from all bishops in the Roman Catholic Cathedral Church, what would be shown me by the spirit, I understood my extraordinary mission; although I did not know, what the Heavenly Congress intended to perform by my mediumship. And when I was commanded by the spirit at 1 o'clock from Monday to Tuesday before Easter 1838, to arise and to write for the book, which is now called the first of my five German volumes, I felt more than before the importance of the obligations of the 144 witnesses who have signed their names in my catalogue; and from this view I wrote that night what I inserted in the most suitable place of the manuscript, that it was then published for a testimony to all nations, that I did know nothing in regard to the deepest mystery which was intended by the Heavenly Congress with that excommunication.

One point more as preparation for the great celebration of the Easter Sunday, April 15, 1838. On Wednesday before Easterthe man who was excommunicated on Sunday Quinquagesima from our congregation, came to me after having separated from the woman with whom he was not married. I understood that he was under influence of an invisible power brought to me, and that I had to take him into our communion and make it publicly known on Easter Sunday in the same general terms without mentioning his name, in which he was separated. And I said to him, that I will mention this in our next meeting on Easter Sunday.

When all was prepared on that great Easter Sunday, in the midst of our usual prophetical performances at the Mass I ascended the pulpit and delivered under inspiration a sermon preparatory to the excommunication, instructed the audience then regarding the excommunicated by a distinct report, how I was three times ordered to perform that excommunication, that therefore those who are comprehended under the names of the excommunication, are as certainly excommunicated from Christ's Church, as I am confirmed as his messenger for establishing his reign of Truth and Justice, Harmony and Peace on the whole Globe by all the signs and wonders many of which they had already heard in my addresses, others they will read in the book. The congregation knew, that I was printing a book in Cambridge near Boston, showing that what I was doing I was doing under the direction of Heavenly messengers for the fulfilment of the greatest promises. Amongst all the signs and wonders many of which you have also read in this book, one of the most remarkable signs was, that after my having excommunicated Benedict Fenwick, Bishop of Boston, in both letters, that of the 16th as well as that of the 17th February 1838, although more expressedly in the last than in the first, neither the Bishop nor any other Priest did interfere with my using the Roman Catholic Cathedral Church of Boston, but I performed without the least disturbance all that has been shown to me by the holy martyr Revel. xiv: 14 and his company. I assured the congregation at the same time that the excommunication will not injure those who are comprehended in the names of the excommunicated, except if they remain obstinate after the excommunication is made known.

After the necessary solemn preparation, the excommunication was performed in the most vigorous manner, and the names of the excommunicated were read so loud and distinctly, that they could be heard in every corner of the church, for the peculiar purpose that no name might be confounded with another name.

After that act I continued the Mass and distributed the Eucharist to a large number of the congregation whom I prepared on the previous days by hearing their confessions; because, as I have mentioned before, in my extraordinary mission in the Roman Catholic Cathedral Church all that which was practised was to be repeated for a testimony that it was accomplished. Without there being room here to write about the confession we mark only in general, that it had also its time in the old Heaven, but we have better means of education in the new Heaven. But it is to be remarked that also the man who had been excommunicated on Sunday Quinquagesima, came to me to the confession before Easter and was received into our congregation, and this was then on Easter Sunday directly after my solemn sermon before I commenced to prepare the audience for hearing the excommunication of those who were to be excommunicated, distinctly announced to the congregation, and that same man received then with the others the Eucharist from my hand. Then he, after our service, accompanied me closely, without saying a word, to my lodging, and said when I was entering the house, that he wished to talk with me privately. When we were alone, he entreated me pitifully to receive him in Christ's Church or in our congregation. I was surprised, and asked him, whether he forgot, that I received him first privately, and whether he did not hear that I made that known to the congregation on that same day, and that he took also the Eucharist from my hand as the confirmation of being in our congregation. He replied that all this was true, but that he heard distinctly his name, when I read those who were excommunicated, and that the Spirit said to him, that he should go directly to me and tell me this.

I saw that he was acting under the influence of a spirit, and to get some more information, asked him, how he could hear his name, when I pronounced loud and distinctly those who were on my paper for the excommunication, when I read them from the paper as being excommunicated, and that I could not be such a fool as to put the same name amongst the excommunicated, whom I took before privately into our Communion, and announced this also publicly, immediately before the performance of the excommunication. He replied, that he did not only hear distinctly his name, but saw it also on the paper from which I read those who were excommunicated, and if I would show him the paper, on which those are who were excommunicated, he would show me his name. Neither he nor any other man could read the names from that paper, which I had in the New Testament book, in my pocket, and from which I read to the audience, what was to be read from that book on Easter Sunday; but my pulpit was so arranged, that nobody besides me could see what I read. When he demanded to see that paper, to show me his name, I took the paper from that book, to satisfy him, that he was mistaken. As soon as I had shown him the paper, he fixed his finger to a name and exclaimed: "This is my name! this is my name!" The more I assured him, that he was mistaken and that he should look better the letters of the name, to see that it was not his but quite another name, the more he affirmed, that it was his name; and the more he looked at the name, the more he asserted, that it was his name. Then I named each letter of that name, asking him, whether he saw that it was the named letter, and when he answered in the affirmative to all letters, I urged him to spell the whole name. And he spelt the whole name, and it was "Kaiser." This German name means in English "Emperor."

As soon as the man, or rather the departed spirit who urged him, that he performed all this, spelt the name Kaiser, that is, Emperor, the spirit seemed to be quite satisfied. After a short pause he again operated upon the man powerfully, saying, that he had brought his name on the 7th Jan. into my catalogue. I understood always, that he meant that man whose name was Kaiser, and I said, that his name is not in the catalogue. But when he continued to assert, that it is in the catalogue, and I repeated that I perused oftentimes that catalogue and was quite certain, that his name is not in the catalogue, and we both remained, each on his point of certainty, I said at length, ,that I would convince him, that I was correct, if he would tell me, who was the next before him, who put his name in the catalogue. And when he named him and also others before and after him, I opened the catalogue, and saw, that on the 100th place, which was according to that direction his place, was the name "Kaiser," that means "Emperor," instead of the name "Geyer" that means "hawk" or "vulture." Geyer was the name of the man who had brought on the 7th January, 1838, instead of his own, the name Kaiser. But by all our precautions, that there might not be a mistake in any name and by all our uses of that catalogue until that moment no body discovered this!

That my business with that man required more time than could be spared, because others were waiting till I dispatched him, and then all that Easter Sunday there was other work so that I had no time to reflect upon that case, nor, if there had been time, had I dared to think, what might have been behind the vail, without having received peculiar revelation. Having been occupied on that Easter Sunday with other business as well as with hearing confessions of those who came from far, I was then tired and went to rest. During my rest I was awakened by an Angel of the Lord, and heard the voice, that I should arise and write a communication. I arose, kindled a light and saw by the watch, that it was one o'clock after midnight, and felt that there was a company of Spirits present, while I received from one the communication which was to be delivered on that day to the congregation. That was the second day of Easter, a festival in the Roman Catholic Church, and we had our service. That communication not belonging into this epitome, was mentioned, because it was a preparation to what follows.

After having finished writing that communication between 1 and 2 o'clock, A. M. on Easter Monday, April 16, 1838, I felt much stronger than at the receipt of the first communication that I was surrounded by a company of Spirits, amongst whom, at that moment, my mother approached next to me, and with an unexpected power of her voice which made such an impression upon my spirit and my whole system as may be easier felt than expressed with words, delivered the message that, I received in our ecclesiastical communion the man who directed my attention to the Emperor who was excommunicated, and that that Emperor was excommunicated who pretends to be Apostolic Majesty, and that I must write down this and publish in the book which was at that time in composition.

I mentioned above, that I received by my departed mother one communication twelve years before that; and this was the second and also until this hour the last communication which I have received by the instrumentality of my mother. Never in my life, at all my experience from the Spirit world, I was so affected as at that communication. It was delivered after having written the first communication, and thought to extinguish the light and return to bed. At that moment I felt that I was surrounded by a company of Heavenly Messengers amongst whom one was approaching nearest, and the powerful communication came. After that there was no inclination to return to bed, nor is there room here to repeat, what has been explained in the first and second of my five often mentioned German volumes, for the correct understanding of said communication, and the prophecies which have been fulfilled in said excommunication and explained in my third volume. From those explanations it is evident, that the Emperor of Austria who has besides other anti-Christian titles also the title "Apostolic Majesty," is representing in that excommunication the whole body of Monarchs and Tyrants, who keep people in the anti-Christian servitude, from which they are to be redeemed at the present manifestation of Christ by his Messengers.

Since the female sex has been mnch more injured and abused by monarchs and other tyrants than the masculine sex, Beatrice Dante's departed wife was found as most suitable Heavenly messenger by whom the great prophecy in the 33d and last Song of Purgatory was communicated to the Poet and most remarkable Prophet Dante, aud my mother was found most suitable to deliver the above mentioned communication and to make greater impression than any other Heavenly messenger upon me, when the first message was to be delivered to understand that great prophecy and thousands of other prophecies which have been locked until that time. At that moment a key was given to commence to unlock them.

We give only some hints regarding the points which are the substance of the contents of the five Germam volumes published from 1838 to 1842; and many volumes would be required, if we would explain the memorable events which happened afterwards for new illustrations and confirmations of the preceding events. There is a concatenation of the most solemn warnings to all the upholders and supporters of the old ruined Babylon, that they should come out not to be partakers of her plagues. Besides the mentioned mystery on the 100th place of our catalogue there is another mystery on the 90th place. Besides those two, four or five others as you may read the whole report in those volumes, have neglected to fulfil their highest duty, and were excommunicated on Easter Sunday, 1838. But those four or five came after that excommunication to me and were received in our communion; but the 90th and the 100th have been brought by their mediums for the fulfilment of prophecies and for the most solemn divine assurance to political and ecclesiastical rulers, that they are in such a tremendous condition, in which they would not remain a moment, but would become directly with us messengers of Peace, if they would comprehend but a little of what we know regarding their condition.

After having received such an astonishing unexpected light regarding the 100th of the 144 witnesses of our catalogue, that only those can duly appreciate it who have studied my volumes, others who have neglected their duty and came in the number of the excommunicated only for an illustration of those on the 90th and 100th places, as we have explained in those volumes, came then without having been called, to me, and were received in our communion. But the 90th did not come, and his place and his names had a peculiar reference to all that which has been performed in the Cathedral Church of Boston by our instrumentality; but I had received no communication in regard to him. Therefore I thought proper to send Messengers to inquire, whether anybody knew a man having the name "Leo Hefner" and having been in Boston at the time in which the 144 witnesses signed their names in my catalogue. But after the most careful inquiry nobody brought any account of Leo Hefner. After that I received the communication, that that name which is on the 90th place of our catalogue, is a mystery which must be explained by me.

Then I commenced to explain, that most suitable names have been selected by Divine wisdom for the excommunication of the Beast which has the mouth of a Leo, that means in English a Lion, Revelation, xiii: 2, and the Beast is the Papal Monarchy, for the foundation of which although several predecessors of Pope Leo I. were preparing the way, that Leo or Lion contributed most by his energy and principles which are expressed in his writings, to that monarchy, which afterwards Pope Gregory VII. endeavoured to establish with great power, and his successors triumphed at length against their adversaries, and the mouth of these lions under the christian mask swallowed as much of human life and property as it could reach, and the whole succession or family of the Popes produced a "Hefner." In the explanation of the expressive names which have been prepared by the Heavenly Congress, we take the most suitable significations which appear obviously in the names. We took the name "Hefner" as a composition of German Hef or Hefe, which means "dregs" or "sediment," and the Hebrew "Ner," which means Lamp, so that Hefner means "dregs of the Lamp" in our interpretation. The Pope used the Hebrew Lamp and besides others especially German scholars gave him the greatest assistance, that by his anti-christian management the Lamp of Truth and Righteousness could not burn, because there was oil consumed and dregs of the most dreadful materialism were destroying and ruining mankind.

It is to be understood, that we give only some hints of what we explained in the first volume as far as our leaders found proper to do, showing gradually the great apostasy from the christian truth and immersion into materialism and ceremonialism, produced by the anti-christian mangement of the " Hefner or Dregs of the Lamp." In the second volume we cotinued the explanation, that is, I under the direction of invisible agents, was writing for the second volume. When I thought that regarding the Beast with ten Horns was sufficient explanation given for that volume, I heard on the 20th November, 1838 at noon time a Heavenly voice : " Count the number of the name of the Beast." Revelation, xiii : 17 and 18. I replied " Lord ! I counted it long time ago.' Then the Heavenly voice was repeated. I asked, " Is'nt Lateinos " the right name? I received the answer : No. Then I understood, that neither that name which was delivered by the old Church Father Irenaeus and written with Greek letters gives the number 666 and points to the affairs of the Latin Man, nor any other name found for an illustration of the prophecy and containing 666, expresses what is prophesied about the beast ; but that Hefner contains the whole mystery ; because each pope as pope has the mouth of a leo or lion, and the whole family or succession of the popes have produced the Hefner, or dregs in the lamp, which cannot burn, because oil is consumed with the mouth of the Leo. After my having explained for the second volume, that all circumstances testified that by " Leo Hefner " the Papal Monarchy was excommunicated from Christ's Church, and that in this name the whole history of Popery is comprehended, showing what every pope as pope is, and what the whole succession of the popes had poduced, the heavenly voice " Count the number of the name of the beast," has given the most striking divine confirmation or divine seal to our interpretation of the mystery. I wrote the family name, after having received the heavenly order, with Greek letters, and to my astonishment they gave exactly the number 666, Revel. xiii : 18. Greek scholars should keep in mind, that the German H is expressed by the Greek mark which is called by grammarians spiritus asper, and that in both syllables of Hefner *e* is long, and with this remark they will find by writing Hefner with Greek letters, in the name exactly the number 666.

After having received the Heavenly order, that I counted

the number of the beast, while I was writing the manuscript and preparing the print of the second volume in Philadelphia, I received soon a letter from Boston containing the information, that Matthew Arnold who is on the 86th place of the 144 witnesses and in the deputation who after my having excommunicated Bishop Benedict Fenwick from my ecclesiastical communion, came to move me to occupy the church for my performances, was inspired and remained when the other left my room when I received the communication to occupy the church for our work, that same man learned who the man was who brought the name Leo Hefner into my catalogue. Since there were usually besides the witnesses also a number of others in the school room, in which names were signed in my catalogue, it seemed to be an easy task to discover the man, who had brought the name, by asking those who signed their names next the 90th. But there are thousands of discoveries quite easy, but they could not be made, till the time for their use arrived. Besides me, all the 144 were also under so strict a control of invisible agents, that all happened in due time. After all other things regarding the mystery have been disclosed and also the number of the beast has been counted, I received the information, that the man who has brought the name, was a single man, quite suitable that he became a medium of Pope Leo xii. The first name of that medium was not Leo, but he was known under the French name Louis, although his German name was Ludwig ; and his family name was Hefner. But Leo Hefner was not his name. He was brought as a medium of the departed Pope Leo XII. and he gave the name which we needed. His family name corresponded with the whole mystery of the fruits of the family or succession of the Popes, but he was only a medium, and instead of his proper name a name was to be given which suited the mystery, and the Pope amongst the departed who represented the succession of the Popes, had to give his own name. Here is no room to repeat the explanation from my often mentioned volumes, how tangibly it was shown by signs, that Pope Leo XII. was the leader who had brought that medium for the most astonishing excommunication of popery. The name Leo has given also the stopping place, from which we count in different directions the epochs of the duration of the Papal monarchy. We have done so in the third German volume and in the work which exists in Latin, German and English for our monthly theological course and for the Latin convention, if the Emperors of France and Austria comprehend us and call their bishops together, to learn the great things which are disclosed for the pacification of the world. Bible Students may explain many things by the hints, given in this book, for instance, how the three verses of the 18th chapter of the Revelation have been fulfilled on Easter Sunday, April, 15, 1838, by the excommunication of the Beast and its image or its ten Horns from Christ's Church. We could name here the powerful Angel, Revelation, xviii : 1. But here is no room to explain, why that martyr was found most qualified for that office, that he delivered to me three times the command to perform that excommunicatiom, in which the proclamation is included : "Babylon the great is fallen, is fallen, and is become the habitation of demons, and the hold of every foul beast, and a cage of every unclean and hateful bird." Revelation, xviii : 2. Interpreters did not know, how to read the text, because some manuscripts have the word "beast" and others have instead of that word "spirit." But the powerful Angel who had the superintendency in these affairs, has shown, that you have to read the word "Beast," because he has given to Pope Leo XII. the order to inspire his medium, to give for our use the name "Leo," or Lion who is the king amongst the Beasts, for our use in the excommunication of the Papal monarchy from Christ's Church, and the medium, although of German parents, was secreted under the French name Louis, in reference to the French Kings, who were for a great support, and at length for a great fall of popery.

But with the Imperial Family of Austria is an other phase. "Petra dedit Petro et Petrus Diadema Rudolpho." This was the motto when the infernal holiness inspired the Pope, to send the crown to the Count of Hapsburgh, to have that count when he becomes Emperor of Germany, his obedient servant. At length, after the support of all kinds of Papal Imperial Royal abominations the departed Emperor Francis was allowed to take the most suitable medium in

possession. The proper name of the medium should have been Eagle according to the delight of Emperors in that Fowl. But our superintendent in those affairs took rather the Hawk or Vulture as a more suitable rapacious fowl, who put the name Emperor instead of his name into our catalogue. That the departed Emperor Francis of Austria became the leader of that his medium, will be shown below for a peculiar instruction of Emperor Francis Joseph, that he might become with us messenger of the New Era. But before this we must give here a very brief lesson to Pope Pius IX, although this whole book and especialy this treatise contain extraordinary lessons for him, and we could write a large volume of correspondences of wonders and signs in Pope Pious IX actions with our apostolic actions.
Bishops would have converted long time ago Pope Pius IX into a powerful preacher of the New Era if they themselves had studied our message of Peace, or rather the Papal monarchy would have been extinguished long time before the appearance of Pope Pius IX. Gregory XVI was the last Pope in the ordinary course of affairs. While I was reading his book: "Il trionfo della Santa Sede e della Chiesa" (the triumph of the Holy See and of the Church,) my Lord has opened my eyes, that he was near to overthrow the See of his infernal holiness, supported by such an abominable delusion as is contained in that pestilential book and other similar impositions. But I did not know at that time, by what kind of means it would be effected, till A. D. 1838 the wonderful works were executed in the Cathedral Church of Boston, so that I expected, that bishops would, after the publication of my explanation of those events, comprehend them and instruct their Pope in what was his highest duty. But they proved to be miserable servants of this their grandmaster of abominations.

Popes with their whole Hierarchy are continuously repeating prophecies and at the same time refusing to do what is their highest duty for the fulfilment of prophecies. I could not have expected, that Pope Gregory XVI, that machine of darkness, would have paid attention, if I had applied directly to him. But if bishops had studied our writings and comprehended our mission and its credentials, they might have drawn also their master Gregory XVI, to look into our matters. But he vegetated and died in the fulness of his prophetical position, whereas he was not ready to enter into the Dispensation of the fulness of times, Ephes. 1 : 10, which is to be introduced by messengers whom I represent. I mentioned that the whole Papal Church is prophetical. In her is concentrated the prophecy of Judaism and Heathenism. Popes who had a peculiar charge, had also names and numbers correspondent to their charge. When in Pope Leo XII the apostolic number was complete he prophesied, as readers must recollect, according to his Leonine wisdom about a Church Doctor or Apostle of the higher mission, and after his departure he had to inspire and bring the man into our school-room, to sign the most suitable-mysteries on the 90th place of our catalogue for the excommunication of Popery from Christ's Church. And Pope Gregory XVI had to write the above quoted book, while he was yet a monk. But by that book the way was opened for him to the Papal Chair. He prophesied on the title-page of that book in the first place the triumph of the Holy See or the Papal Government. And it triumphed so, when he became Pope that with his successor the whole miserable machinery is breaking and breaking, till at length the Church, that is, the people will triumph by receiving our message of Peace, by which all kinds of Popery will be abolished from the Globe. He on the Papal Chair concentrated in his name and number of the name the whole mystery of his position. He was Gregory, that means a watchman, as prophets are called, and he stands as prophet, in the full number XVI, which is as remarkable in the developments of Popery as the number 666, so that the disciples of the Revelator were debating, whether the spirit had given to their master the number 666, or the number 16 in Revel. xiii : 18, till the spirit had shown by our instrumentality, that the number 666 is the principal number in counting the name and the periods of the duration of the government of that Beast, but the number 16 comprehends many of its deep mysteries. The 4th Beast in the 7th chapter of Daniel was formed gradually into the shape of the Papal monarchy, and 4 times 4 is the complete number in which the last ordinary Pope appeared in his glory ; he is the "infallible monarch of the church," as he himself has proved while he was yet a monk, in the above quoted book, that the Pope is the infallible monarch of the church. By the means of that book my Lord of truth and righteousness has opened my eyes, that I commenced to comprehend the infernal imposition of the dragon and his host, by which nations were so duped that they believed the Papal infallibility, holiness and all other abominations and blasphemies of the living God and his Christ, and that I have performed and explained what is required for the abolition of all kinds of Popery. The number of the Biblical writing mediums or prophets, whose books are collected in one section of the books of the Old Testament, is sixteen. They were as little understood as to who they were and where they were, as the Popes. The number of the Popes each of whom appears under the name Gregory or watchman, is also sixteen, or two times eight. The last of them or the sixteenth Gregory was the Pope under whose administration the mysteries were performed by our instrumentality for the abolition of all kinds of popery. But he continued to rule in all his glory and to keep disturbers of his infallible monarchy in prison. He was the most glorious during the time, in which the Beast or the Papal monarchy is in the number eight, Revelation, xvii : 11.

The often mentioned catalogue of the 144 witnesses which appears in the English translation of my 4th German volume, entitled "The one thing needful," from the 533d till 538th page, is a concentration of wonders and signs, which were effected under the control of the 144,000 martyrs, Revelation xiv : 1. In reference to this mystery as well as in reference to the 144 cubits of the wall of the New Jerusalem, Revelation, xxi : 17, their number is exactly 144. They were the stones used while we were performing in the Roman Catholic Cathedral Church what was required according to prophecies for the removal of Babylon and bilding of the New Jerusalem. "Behold I come as a thief." Revelation xvi : 15. He came so secretly, that neither on the 7th Jan., 1838, while those 144 witnesses were signing their names into my catalogue nor afterwards, while they were performing each his task, we understood much of what was behind the vail, till after the great excommunication on Easter

Sunday, 1838, the great mystery commenced gradually to be developed, and I received on the third Sunday after Easter, 1838, directly before the service, from my guardian the direction to deliver the valedictory sermon in order that all which was to be executed in that church according to prophecies, had been accomplished. The church had prepared for our use on that Sunday the 16th chapter of John. And I selected the text: "A little while, and ye shall not see me: and again a little while and ye shall see me, because I go to the Father. John, xvi: 16.

If you have comprehended this book to this page, you know, that I am Jesus Christ's first-born son in the Dispensation of the Fullness of Times. Ephes. 1: 10. But also after having been publicly initiated to this ministry on Sunday Sexagesima, February 18th, 1838, at the altar of the Cathedral Church of Boston, I progressed slowly in the development of the mystery.

All disclosures which I give are preparatory for an easier understanding of the great testimony of the three witnesses named at the caption of this treatise. I am partly going around and applying to all kinds of mediums in the cities of New York and Brooklyn, and in all directions is somewhat prepared for an illustration of the testimony of the three extraordinary witnesses. On Sunday, 24th inst., when the message of "the Treaty of Peace" between the Emperors of Austria and France arrived in America but was not communicated to us on that day, I wrote some of the last disclosures before this paragraph. After that I wrote two letters. But before having finished the second, I was inspired to go and I thought that I was going to a Conference meeting of Spiritualists; but on my way I met with one who is holding his own meetings publicly to draw the incautious into private "Free Love Meetings," and I went with him to his public meeting. When I returned to my room I was tired, went to bed, and then I arose yesterday, July 25th, and finished at fish-oil light the second letter of July 24th, 1859. Then I wrote three other letters before breakfast, at which I heard the first report of "the Peace Treaty." After that I was occupied all day in the cities of New York and Brooklyn. I thought proper, to write this episode this morning, July

26th, before my starting to other business; because it is in such a connexion with the "Peace Treaty," that it will be in the proper place more particularly explained for a great illustration of the three extra-ordinary witnesses.

"Christ's first-born Son in the Dispensation of Universal Harmony and Peace on the whole globe" is the third angel preaching powerfully in the 9th, 10th and 11th verses of the 14th chapter of the Revelation. There have been a number of prophecies which have been referred to Christ who has been crucified by the Jews more than eighteen hundred years ago, but which cannot be understood except in regard to his first-born son and the whole Body of Messengers whom he represents. Since our public appearance some mediums have preached that now Christ's first-born son appears, and were quoting a number of Biblical passages testifying this. If there would be room, I would write some pages regarding my meetings in Cincinnati of Ohio with the principal of those mediums. He after having been an elder in the Mormon Church, separated from them and was preaching "the Judgment Dispensation," and that Christ's first-born Son was coming now. Although my meetings with that prophet would be for a peculiar illustration of the testimony of the three extraordinary witnesses, I can mention here only the substance, that he was often times possesed by some of the generals of Napoleon I. to give from his position peculiar testimonies to our mission. Once, for instance, was he so strongly inspired by his leader, that he wrote a decree by the authority of that his god, in which he appointed me to be "Pope Andrew I." It was A. D. 1846. He gave a copy of that decree to an editor of a newspaper in Cincinnati,—to the same who publishes now in Washington City the National Era, which will be used before the close of this treatise in a peculiar connexion with the three witnesses, and he handed to me a copy of the same decree. At the perusal of that decree I saw that a dragon was the god by whom he was inspired, and I wrote directy a protest, to accept any office from his God who was a spirit of delusion and destruction. I handed my protest to the same editor with the remark that if he publishes the appointment for me to be Pope Andrew I, he must publish also my protest. He made known this to that medium who under those circumstances withdrew the decree. He was a rich general, and there is no doubt, that as Pope in a new shape I had found soon support of other rich persons to carry out the plan of the dragon for destruction.

While I was writing the 4th of the five often mentioned German volumes I had to quote oftentimes the catalogue of the 144 witnesses, and was continuously aware, that not only the 90th, and the 100th, who have brought as Mediums not their own names but the names which were suitable to the office of those, by whom they were inspired, obtained the places which according to our language by numbers were most suitable to the mystery which they contain, but that also those who have brought their own names, brought them as mediums of invisible agents by whom they were controlled in such a manner, that those who had peculiar charges, obtained also the places with numbers corresponding to their charges. After having observed many times this phenomenon I saw at length the necessity of publishing that catalogue with the names in the same order, in which they had been brought into the catalogue. But at that time I was not aware, that the catalogue contains exactly 144 witnesses. the complete mystical number of their represensation; because on the 538th page of " the One Thing needful " that catalogue ends with " 143 Anthony Larger," and in my first three volumes as well as in " The One thing Needful " or in the 4th volume these witnesses are named " the 143 witnesses." On the 538th page the paragraph after the close of that catalogue commences: " This is the foundation catalogue of the new reign of Christ on earth," and in the same paragraph these witnesses are called the 143 witnesses; because they occupy 143 places, and I was not aware that there were 144 witnesses in that catalogue, till at length I heard the voice: " Count exactly the number of the witnesses." I looked then at every place, and found that on each place of the catalogue is only one witness, except the 81st place in which are two sisters together, and therefore the number of witnesses in that catalogue is 144 in reference to the 144,000 members of the Heavenly Congress Revelation xiv: 1, by whose wisdom names for that catalogue were wonderfully provided, and in reference to the 144 cubits of the measure of the walls of the New Jerusalem, Revelation xxi: 17, the chief corner stone of which being Jesus Christ, and the members of his peaceable kingdom are named lively stones. 1 Peter ii: 5. And ,those 144 were given to me as assistants to show what is to be done for the establishment of Christ's peaceable reign on earth, to wit, all the ecclesiastical and political powers must co-operate with us to draw all nations into the new era. Here we give only some hints, how wonderfully they are exhorted and urged by all other events, as well as by the formation of that catalogue in which is the concentration of wonders and signs.

We quote the following places from the catalogue as peculiar instances in reference to the three "extra-ordinary witnesses: "80, Bischofberger with two, 81 sisters." This man came under the strong control of his guardian, and when the quoted words were signed, and on the place "81 sisters" appeared, we required the names of his sisters. But he said, the names will be made known to me another time. Each signer had to give his name, but Bischofberger after having put the name "sisters" on the 81st place of the catalogue, refused to give their names, and assured me that they will be made known in due time, and I received orders from my leader to let it remain as it was written. When the unexpected wonders which are concealed in that catalogue, commenced to be disclosed, it was manifest, that on the 80th place was put the representative of the Beast which itself is the eighth king, Revelation xvii: 11 and has ten horns. To show, that it was in the complete age or in the fulness of its glory in our age, it was put on the ten times the eighth place with suitable names. To wit, Alexis means one who hinders. He hinders the redemption of mankind from oppression and the development of truth and justice, which is required for this redemption. And the family name shows who this man is, to wit, "Bischofberger." The first part of this compound name is the same word, as the English word "Bishop," and the German "Berge" are "Mountains," so that this Bishop is Bishop of the Mountains, or on the Mountains, having his seat on the mountains, in reference to the seven mountains on which Rome is located. In this his glory he has two sisters, which represent the two powers of the Pope, to wit, the ecclesiastical and political power. He himself in his glory and both his powers have been typified on the 80th and 81st places of our catalogue showing to the Pope his highest duty, to become with us messenger of Christ's peaceable reign.

On the six places which precede immediately the 80th place, those are represented who have raised the Pope so high as he stands. We remark, that the German name Ochs is pronounced as the English name Ox and means the same beast. Those representatives are in our catalogue in the following order: 74 Joseph Ochs, 75 Conrad Ochs. 76 Aloysius Ochs. 77 John Ochs. 78 Iidorus Ochs. 79 Joseph Januarius Ochs. The number six is the fundamental number of the number of the name of the Beast 666, Revelation xiii: 18, and to one or the other of the six classes of men who appear here as oxen, all orders of monks may be reduced. The name which stands before the name "Ochs," defines nearer the position of the representative Ochs. Monks of all Papal orders appear in reference to the Pope as Oxen, tame useful animals, working for the support of Popery, without knowledge of their own and the true condition of the Pope. But Revelation xiii: 11 we read: "I beheld another beast coming up out of the earth, and he had two horns like a lamb, and he spake as a dragon." Here are the orders of monks under the image of a Therion, a ferocious beast, which appears as a lamb to those whom it entraps for the Pope, but it is ferocious, although it hides its ferocity, as a dragon, till its delusion is made manifest, when it destroys the enemies of the Pope. It is caught in all six shapes into our catalogue, the explanation of the mysteries of which in our volumes shows to all monks and priests the urgent necessity to become with us messengers of the new era And the explanation from the 11th verse to the end of the 13th chapter of the Revelation and of other mysteries is in our volumes showing the dreadful condition of monks and priests in their present course.

We have given some hints without explanations which are in my printed volumes and in the manuscript, which

N. B. On this great prophetical Feast, August 15, 1859, of Mary's Assumption into Heaven and of Napoleon I's Birthday, I mention that I was since the twenty-first day of June last, on which day agreement was made with the printer and the manuscript of the First Treatise was given him for printing this book, confined to New York, wishing to have it printed as soon as possible. But those Messengers from our sphere who have the commission to count according to our spirit language by numbers, pages and lines in my publications and days for their printing in agreement with the calendar, for this purpose controlling the spirits of the compositors, did not hinder them to annoy me in manifold ways. At length I wrote on the 1st inst. my complaint and carried it to the same attorney who without charge wrote the agreement; but not having found him in his office, I myself carried it to the printer, expecting a good effect. But I was as much disappointed, as when I commenced to write the Fourth Treatise and thought that it would not become larger than the largest of the preceding Treatises. But having become more than twice as large, we stopped the composition of the Fourth Treatise at the end of the 168th page, which according to the printer's calculation will be finished on the 17th inst. The portion of the Fourth Treatise which appears in this edition is a necessary preparation to comprehend the proper position of Pope Pius IX. and of the Emperors of France and Austria, and to understand the mysteries of the dates of the remarkable events in the last war in Italy. Those dates testify that those events happened under strict control of our leaders watching the infernal furies destroying men, and in so exact a correspondence with events of our mission, that if you comprehend this book and act accordingly, you will open soon the door for the New Era in America and in Europe; but if you neglect this the three extraordinary witnesses have such a position as to continue judgments.

Those who comprehend this book, will be anxious to read also the continuation and the end of the Fourth Treatise, and will collect as many subscribers as possible. As soon as they secure us to call a printer to our Peace Union Centre and to publish a new edition of this book, we will send gratis to them in an extra pamphlet the "Supplement to the

Fourth Treatise," which will appear in the next edition. Therefore we request those who buy this book, to give their exact direction either to those from whom they buy or to send it according to the direction on the title-page.

ANDREW B. SMOLNIKAR.

FIFTH TREATISE.

The Plan for Redemption of Nations from monarchical and other oppressive speculations and for the introduction of the promised New Era of Harmony, Truth and Righteousness on the whole globe.

We write the following pages only for those who have studied all the preceding pages of this book, and concentrate the subject of what would require volumes, on few pages, to be gradually developed in our Periodical. On the title-page of this book our Mission is expressed, and the four preceding Treatises contain superabundance of credentials or testimonials of our mission as well as the great truth, that the social, political and ecclesiastical relations of mankind are rotten and corrupt, the whole structure is a Babylon, confusion and delusion, which is to be abolished and on its place truth and justice, harmony and peace are to be established by virtue of our mission.

Readers of this book know that I speak as medium of messengers from the Heavenly Congress who have the commission to introduce the New Era, and as representative of messengers by whom nations are to be moved for action to escape from the plagues which continue in the ruins of Babylon till people come out and establish the New Jerusalem, the new order of things, in which persons of both sexes will receive such development of their intellectual and moral faculties and of their physical skill and strength as they will be qualified to receive, to enjoy themselves in their mortal bodies as well as after their departure such happiness as their persons will be capable of enjoying while they themselves will contribute, each member his or her share to the common welfare of mankind, that the whole society will progress as far as circumstances will allow.

This development demands time. It could not take place in a moment, but means which have been in preparation and prepared through the course of ages may be concentrated, and when thus concentrated they may be usefully applied in accelerating the true and right education of degraded humanity, and in a few years that may be effected, which past centuries did not effect. But with all the knowledge which we have acquired for promoting the true happiness of mankind, we can do nothing for them, if they are not reached and aroused from their lethargy. If they will be redeemed from their present miserable and wretched condition, they must begin to comprehend where they are and to what point of intellectual and moral perfection with corresponding happiness and health and strength of body and mind they could arrive, if they would apply their energy and the means which are prepared by nature as well as by human skill, art and science to be used in bringing mankind from their present Babylon or from the existing confusion and delusion into the new Jerusalem, into the New Era, into the new order of things, which is usually called the Millennium, about which there are many false and wrong notions, but which will be the universal republic in which truth and righteousness will reign and all nations will be united in the great brotherhood in which they will enjoy perpetual peace. We have received the commission and the credentials of the Mission to introduce this state of things.

To commence with power the grand work which is to be acoomplished by co-operation of men and women, who are associated amongst themselves and united with Heavenly messengers who are commissioned to prepare for the promised New Era, we unite and form an Association which we call Peace-Union (Friedens-Verein), a union of co-operation for establishing peace. Real, perpetual peace comprehends the restoration of human rights. Our co-operation for this purpose needs a centre, a place on which we concentrate the means to attain our object. Hence, we according to our mission, invite all who are able to contribute their share, either in money or property or any kind of mental and physical labor for the realization of the object, that they might cooperate with us to establish first a centre of our work, and according to the pattern of the centre as many other settlements as may be required for accommodation of all who would enter into the New Era.

The first centre should be a provisional centre, that is, a place for concentrating our co-operation so long as may be necessary, till for the same purpose a more suitable place be furnished. But not all who are invited to co-operate, can have accommodation on the first central station, nor would all be ready at once, who might so desire, if buildings and other necessary conveniences were provided, which, however, is primarely to be attended to. We need co-operators everywhere to arouse as many as can be aroused for co-operation with us in these days of Noah, at the approach of the flood of tribulations. In my former publications as well as in this book and in my manuscripts a superabundance of credentials are exhibited, that those men and women, who are united with us in Christ's spirit, that is, in the spirit of truth and righteousness, and are living in accordance with what is required by that Spirit, and are spreading the glorious news made manifest by our instrumentality for redemption of oppressed humanity, are true messengers of Christ; but those clergymen who, instead of co-operating with us, are keeping people in shackles of their sects and despising our message of peace, are messengers of the deluding and destroying spirit and supporting the Beast or monarchy which receives its power from the dragon, the deluding and destroying serpent which is the image of that spirit, Revelation xiii: 2. We expect they will comprehend this book and commence to act with all their strength as our fellow-laborers, and become with us partakers of the blessings which will originate from our co-operation.

After this preparation we ask, whether according to the common stock association or according to a true community of goods the centre and other settlements of our Peace-Union should be established. I wrote many years ago a plan according to a common stock association, according to which members of the Peace-Union should have prepared themselves and others for a true community of goods, but within seven years an exact accouut of labor furnished and of its worth as well as of other property should have been kept, and at the expiration of that period the division of profits according to the shares of labor furnished and other property invested should have taken place, and during the period of seven years all the members should have been prepared for the great community or true republic, into which mankind will finally associate, that those who would not be sufficiently prepared before the expiration of seven years to commence a true community, might at least in seven years be prepared for it. At the end of that plan is the paragraph a portion of which we copy here as preparatory to what follows:

"I have mentioned only some of the many points which are to be mentioned in more suitable times, or in the periodical; because that which has been mentioned may suffice to move those who are called and chosen to be the first champions in starting the centre of our action. They may easily comprehend, why we are compelled to commence on so low a station, on which continuous accounts and calculations as well as many other inconveniences will make much trouble. If we would expect good success on a higher ground, we would commence on that ground. But this generation is found in such a degradation and corruption, that also the proposed plan to draw mankind from lower to higher stations, will probably not find directly sufficient support of what we need to bring mankind quickly and powerfully into the New Era, which in its splendor and glory will be the great community of goods, based on true republican principles, &c."

This paragraph was to be copied, because we must give some explanation of the matter, that mankind were to be prepared in manifold ways, to become gragually ready to enter into the right order of things. Readers of this book know, that from A.D. 1838 till 1842 my five German volumes containing "Memorable Events" developing the dreadful social, ecclesiastical and political state of mankind and testifying our mission to introduce the promised New Era, have been published. During and after the publication of those volumes it was evident, that our duty was to make known to those who have read or heard somewhat regarding our mission, that for a powerful co-operation we would need a centre of our action. Adolph Etzler published that time a book entitled: "The New World or Mechanical System to Perform Labour of Man and Beast by Inanimate Powers." I have read it and found the principles correct, and that although all that he proposed, would not be practicable, some of his propositions could be put in practice. And when I saw that Germans were so chained either by materialism or sectarianism, that instead of studying those my five German volumes and of acting accordingly, they followed rather after their sectarian and materialistic leaders who have published all kinds of delusion against my books, and spoke also in a like manner publicly and privately against them, my directors moved me to tell to those who took more or less interest in the contents of my books and were skilful mechanics, that they should study Etzler's book, and if they would find his propositions practicable, they should try to awaken Germans with Etzler's machine to study my German volumes. The best mechanic among them, after having studied Etzler's book, and having seen the draughts of all parts of Etzler's machine and heard Etzler's explanation of all its parts, has assured me in words and in writing that he gave all his property as security, that he would put Etzler's machine in operation. But a seeress who belonged to our association, and gave amongst all women the strongest testimony to our mission, although she did not see the pattern of the machine, received in a vision its whole structure and described exactly the portions which she saw in the vision, that they broke. She received that vision a considerable time before those who were expecting certain success, commenced to build Etzlers machine. I was certain that the prophetical vision would be fulfilled, but I expected that afterwards would be shown how Etzler's mistakes should be repaired, and that great lessons would be given to nations by the trial of that machine, the inventor of which was a great materialist, not knowing that he himself was a strong medium of spirits of a similar character as spirits of Napoleon I. were, to subdue the world by physical means, while I considered that machine as the means of peculiar spirit manifestations to awaken nations from their materialism to our message of peace containing the true spiritualism. The machine was built under Etzler's direction in Warren County, Pa., the trial was made, and the pieces broke which have been foreseen and foretold as breaking.

There was a great jubilee of those who have been deluded by priestcraft, that they thought when Christ was killed, that he would arise no more, When Etzler as well as the man who has given me in words and in writing the pledge with his whole property that he would put the machine in operation, have left the place I said to those who have remained on the place, that in the next night would be revealed to one of them, how the mistakes made by Etzler, should be corrected and the machine should be put in operation. George Karle, a young lame shoemaker, a sincere seeker after truth and firm believer in our mission, was the man to whom the mystery was revealed, and he has explained at our meeting the matter in such a manner, that also those who were most opposed, have at length been convinced, after having heard his explanation how Etzler's mistakes should be repaired, that he had received a true revelation, and agreed that he should be the director in rebuilding Etzler's machine, to make a new trial. But before this has been done, he was brought into the Allegheny River and drowned by the instrumentality of the departed Mormon Prophet Joe Smith, not directly but indirectly by the instrumentality of a cow. But a week after that, on the 30th of July, 1844, the same destroying spirit Joe Smith was allowed to attack me directly, to show how he would be able to kill a man in a minute, if he would be permitted. But he was seized by my guardian and cast into a combustible matter which was by his infernal electricity instantly kindled. George Karle was permitted to be drowned, because the time for establishing our centre had not yet arrived, and Karle had an important mission in the spirit world, and in that great mission he continues to be engaged.

It is to be understood that the given hints regarding Joe Smith would need a peculiar treatise. I did not know him personally in his mortal body, but urged preachers of his sect to move him to meet me either in a written correspondence or personally, to learn to know his dreadful delusion. The same I published in "The one thing needful," and urged his Elders, to send to him an English copy of that volume, which as readers of this book know, has been translated from the German into English. But in that year matters did not yet arrive to maturity for the conversion of Mormon Apostles and Elders. Their infernal President had to show, how his army had the power to prevent my starting the centre of our operation. But that my meeting with the departed Joe Smith occasioned my meeting with the mortal Brigham Young, while he was yet in Nauvoo, but although I preached to him and his disciples the judgment dipensation, they were not yet mature to be converted, and my manuscripts in which dreadful mysteries of the Mormon Spiritualism are developed, must wait to be published, when nations will be prepared to read so important disclosures.

I have given here some hints of my experience at and after the trial of Etzler's machine, by the means of which so much regarding the inner life of man and the spirit world and the dreadful condition of mankind has been disclosed, that volumes would be needed to explain it. That experience is testifying, that time did not yet arrive for establishing the centre. People were ridiculing me and reproaching the machine, not knowing that I have only occasioned its building, and that I warned those who undertook to build it, that they should reflect upon the point, that at its first trial the pieces foretold by the seeres would break, although they would be repaired and the mistake of the inventor corrected, if they would persevere in the work of the Lord. But the wife of the man who undertook the work and gave the pledge, was instigated by Jesuites and their agents and made him blind in the work in which he had to persevere, that by our experience it became at length manifest, that the trial of the machine was made for great instruction of nations. People were deluded by the blind leaders of the blind and would not hear us, when we invited them after the trial for co-operation to establish a centre without trying any machine, but only using machines which have been tried by others and found to be useful. But when we will be in all directions secured with abundant means, we will support inventions for the common welfere.

Here is no room for further explanations, that wherever I endeavoured to start a centre of our co-operation on the plan of the common stock association, great spirit manifestations showing the dreadful condition in the existing Babylon took place, and the inner life of man was more and more developed and all our sufferings have been abundantly rewarded with imperishable treasures. We give here some hints on one case the full explanation of which would need as large a volume as this volume is. During the building of Etzler's machine George Karle found John Zeigler in a hermitage in which he employed one half of his time to chopping wood and the other to studying the Bible and to prepare for a happy home in the spirit world. Karle gave him some instructions regarding our mission and some of my books. Zeigler discovered soon that by studying my books he would receive light which he could not obtain in other ways, and then he studied them deeper than any other mortal man, and whenever his presence was required, he came to give us assistance, and then he returned to his hermitage. In the latter part of 1849 and the commencement of 1850 I was preparing in Indiana and Illinois and especially near the line of both states people for our message and for co-operation to establish on the grand prairie our centre. When I thought to have found the best location for it, I found soon a man of property who paid for the land according to our plan. Then I wrote to J. G. Zeigler who was from his hermitage preparing people by letters for our message, that he should come, and then we would write together to such as we would invite to come as pioneers. He wrote, that he was ready to start directly. He started, but he was pushed into the Ohio River in the night of the 10th of April, 1-50, between 11 and 12 o'clock by a papist instigated by the power of darkness. The whole conspiracy was then detected to us ; but we committed the murderer to the Judgment of the Heavenly Court, and Zeigler continues to work with us amongst the departed. He was an American well versed in English and in German, and his work is extensive. The spirit language by numbers should be known in a certain measure to biblical students ; although the most celebrated amongst them know very little about it. But those who comprehend this book, may easily find out, why I met with the departed Napoleon I. in the 20th line of the 20th page, and why the spirit directed me to repeat this important fact with additional circumstances on the 39th page, and why I meet with Napoleon in the 39th line on the 39th page in this book. Readers in looking into these mysteries should keep in mind, that the battle of Solferino was faught on the same day in the year 1859, on which day I met with Napoleon A. D. 1839. If you understand this book, you will easily comprehend also, why the spirit was pleased to prepare on the same 39th page before the departed Napoleon the departed President Taylor and Buchanan in the Presidential administration, who appears to live although he is yet dead. But his friends should awaken him to study this book and to co-operate with us, that he might escape the judgment in which President Taylor was executed, and John George Zeigler was sent by the Heavenly Congress to give orders to destroying spirits to carry Zach. Taylor into their infernal regions. "Zeigler was the angel of the Lord," mentioned in the first line of the 37th page of this book. He has shown to Zach. Taylor, when he entered from his mortal body into his inner life, my handwriting testifying, that he had neglected to fulfil his highest duty. And I have mentioned in this connexion of things this incident, that you might do what your predecessors have neglected to do.

When by the departure of our martyr John George Zeigler was shown, that the Grand Prairie was not the place for starting our centre, I wrote to the man who has bought and paid for the land, that he was at liberty either to keep that land for his use or to sell it, and then I was preparing in other States people for our message, showing them also the necessity for starting a centre of our cooperation. At lenght at the end of February and at the commencement of March of this year, 1859, was in peculiar manner made manifest, that we should start the "*Centre of our Community,*" or the Centre for establishing the True Republic, which, as has been made manifest, will be a true Community of Goods, and a true matrimony of one man with one woman, as has been prophesied by the first christians at Jerusalem, but could not be accomplished in practice till the dispensation of the fulness of times, Ephes. 1 : 10. or the New Jerusalem will be introduced by messengers whom I represent. If we should find before finishing the last of the 24 pages of the 8th sheet some space, we will give hints on the wonders and signs by which it has been shown, but explanation of these matters must be delayed, till we establish a Printing office at the Centre of our Peace Union Community.

"And fear came upon every soul: and many wonders and signs were done by the Apostles. And all that believed were together, and had all things common. And sold their possessions and goods, and parted them to all men, as every man had need." Acts ii: 43. 44. & 45. "And the multitude of them that believed were of one heart, and of one soul, neither said any of them that aught of the things which he possessed was his own; but they had all things common. Neither was there any among them that lacked: for as many as were possessors of lands or houses sold them, and brought the prices of all things that were sold, and laid them down at the Apostles feet; and distribution was made unto every man according as he had need." Acts iv: 32. 34. & 35.

This was not the commencement of the Community in the Jewish Church, but of the great conversion of those who have been attached to the sects of the Pharisees and the Sadducees. Besides these two sects there was a third sect, called the Esseni or Therapeutes. They understood that the letter of the Jewish Bible kills and that there was in those prophetical books a deeper, a spiritual sense of what was to come, and they retired into the deserts of Egypt, and were acting from thence to convert the world to their community principles. From that association the Christian Religion originated. Jesus Christ was the descendant or offspring of the Therapeutes or Healers, who were powerful in healing diseases of demoniac influence. Their spirittual power came from their strictly moral life, they did not abuse the procreative powers, but those who were married, used them only for obtaining children in the right season, and many of them lived in celibacy in the strictest continence all their life time. Such was the life of the Therapeute Monk Eli or Heli, the Father of Jèsus Christ, Luke 1: 23. He, while living in the strictest celibacy arrived to an advanced age, and when the time arrived for the procreation of the Messiah of the Jews, he became the medium of the spirit who was selected by the Heavenly Congress to seize him and to procreate by his instrumentality the Messiah. And when the departed spirit called Gabriel or the power of God, was operating through Eli that is "My God," Mary was seized by her guardian and submitted, that the offspring was not the origin of a carnal co-operation, but the work of a Holy Spirit, so that Jesus Christ was the concentration of the spiritual power of the highest association amongst the Jews as well as of the prophecy of the Jewish Nation. In one of my former writings I have given more disclosure regarding this mystery, but when we will have our own Printing office, I will give a more complete explanation of the mystery, as well as of my generation, because if you comprehend this book, you know that we have superabundance of signs according to prophecies, by virtue of which I appear as the first born son of Jesus Christ for the introduction of his peaceable reign on earth or the great Community or Republic, for which we must prepare by establishing a centre of our co-operatian.

Here is to be mentioned that regarding the community great abuse was made of the above quoted verses from the above quoted and other biblical passages in monasteries and nunneries as well as in other associations. Christ says to the Angel of the church of Ephesus: " But this thou hast, that thou hatest the deeds of the Nicolaitanes, which I also hate." Revelation, ii: 6. And to the angel of the church in Pergamos he reproaches: " So hast thou also them that hold the doctrine of the Nicolaitanes, which thing I hate." Rev. ii: 15. Nicolaitanes in the Revelation are the same who are in our days known as Free-lovers. Some called them Dr Nichol's people. But that Doctor was at length converted to Romanism, lecturing for the Roman Catholic Church, and the day before yesterday or on the 14th of August, I read the advertisement of his lecturing here in New York. We expect, that he will get this book, comprehend our spiritualism and draw many Roman Catholics into the true Catholic Church, or what is the same, into our Peace Union. Man must be restored to his true condition. A chaste, pure life in celibacy, and a true matrimony in which carnal copulation is usued only for obtaining children when sound reason or the true christian spirit requires it, this is the true condition of man for his true happiness in this and in the future life. All excess in this respect is injurious to body and soul of parents and children. As long as mankind are not reduced to the right order in this repect, they remain in their degradation and misery. How they will be brought to the right order in the true community as the only refuge for the restoration of the human race, will be explained in our Periodical for the common use and particularly to those who will come to our Peace Union, here not being room except to give hints on many points the full explanation of which requires large treatises. Here we give the following hints.

In the present Babylon dollars and cents as the means in this state of affairs used for what man needs to support his mortal life and for committing all kinds of sins and crimes against his fellow men, occupy in so dreadful a manner the minds of men and women in general in their present degraded condition, that the one thing needful, their spiritual progress is so neglected, that probably, if some few comprehend this book so far as to apply all their energy to spread it, they will have a hard task to move the public in general to study it so as it should be studied and comprehended. Reader should recollect, that when I came the first time in my present charge before the public, the passage Luke viii: from the 4th to the 15th verse, was prepared for my use. Besides dollars and cents there are especially the sexual disorders which ruin mankind so, that they appear as dead to the truly spiritual things, for which they will get the right taste, when in the community they comprehend, that mankind belongs to two houses. Americans are quite accustomed to two Houses in the Capitol of Washington; but in the true community they will learn to be accustomed to the two Houses, or two departments in one and the same house, to which mankind belong, when they arrive to the higher perfect order, so that males belong to their own House or department and females to their own, although each husband has his own wife, and each wife her own husband; but they do not meet together for carnal copulation, except in the right season for the only object to get a child, with due preparation to transfuse a holy spirit into the child. Nothing is more injurious to the parents and to the child than the act of procreation without due preparation, which is in this present Babylon generally neglected. Besides this in this present abominable situation of mankind, the act of carnal copulation is oftentimes repeated during the pregnancy and before the child is weaned. All this has a very injurious effect upon the child and degrades and ruins also the parents. Here is no room to explain the hints showing the origin of the hereditary sins, which will be abolished, when the true community will be flourishing, and the whole House of males as well as the whole House of females will support every individual belonging to the House, as well as the whole community in their common meetings will support each other in the progression towards perfection.

These hints may appear quite strange to many readers. But if they will come out from the existing corruption, they may be assured, that they will comprehend me, when I give in a long dissertation a complete explanation of the given hints, in the supposition that those who have comprehended this book know our mission, and that we have received the knowledge which is required to our mission to bring nations out of their present corruption which kills many when they arrive to manhood and womanhood, and many more before that age, and not a small portion of them before or soon after they are born. And all this originates from the corrupt state introduced by the follies of men. When these follies will be removed, mankind in general will commence, within few generations, to become old and will enter into the spirit world with great imperishable riches.

We read : " Verily I say unto you, there is no man that has left house, or brethren, or sisters, or father, or mother, or wife, or children, or lands, for my sake and the gospel's, but he shall receive a hundredfold now in this time, houses and brethren and sisters and mothers and children and lands, ' after persecution,' and in the world to come eternal life." Mark x : 29, 30. According to our reading in the Greek text we translate : " after persecution." When the persecution is abolished, the promised great advantages will be made manifest in the true community. There will not be plurality of wives, but each husband will have his own wife. Now father, mother, wife or children might resist to the determination of a person to join with the true community. Those who comprehend, that this will be the true life in the true reign of Christ, in his Peace-Union, will co-operate with us for its introduction without regard to any opposition of their nearest relatives. Every one who forsakes all and acts with us as much as he can, for establishing the Peace-Union, will when persecution ceases and the Peace-Union flourishes, consider those, who are old, as his fathers and mothers, those of equal age as brothers and sisters, and those who are younger as his children, and all the property belonging to the Peace-Union as ours, and we will truly pray to God: "Our Father."

Not being yet in this happy condition but endeavoring to arouse a general turn towards it, we must make some provisions to support the feeble in their turn, and those who turn towards our Peace-Union that they might easier settle matters with those who belong to their family and will not turn into our Peace-Union.

Every individual who determines to enter into our community, brings all his property into it, after having settled all his business in the world. This property. according to our principles will be taken in possession by the community; and if it is not money but other property, it will be valued according to a very moderate price, and its value and the amount of money if he brings any, will be put into the ledger of the community, and a receipt will be given to him or her under the provisions mentioned as follows: In the possible but not probable case, that he or she should return to the former fashion, the value of the property would be returned, although not directly, but when the community would find easy to do so, In the mean time they would exchange the receipt which he or she received at the delivery of their property, with a note containing the amount of money and the time when the community promise to pay according to the value or course of money at the time received and at the time in which it would be paid to him. For instance, if a dollar received would have at the time in which it would be paid, only the value of ten cents, ten cents would be paid to him or her instead of a dollar, without any interest; because the step should be made after earnest reflection and determination, and with this provision we must deter hypocrites from joining our Peace-Union; but to those who would be feeble, all possible assistance would be given to strenghten them in the work which they would commence. In the true community when it will flourish, everybody will enjoy as much of its riches as is required for his bodily strength and for such an intellectual and moral improvement as to enrich as much his spirit as his faculties will be prepared to receive, that after his departure he or she enters into a happy abode of our Peace Union.

I and other pioneers, who are preparing for the happy state which the Peace-Union community when flourishing will enjoy, must suffer many privations. But the spiritual treasures which during our great struggle with the opposition we acquire, we carry with us at our departure, and where our community will flourish, we will rejoice with them who will partake of the fruits of our labor, so that I will not be less happy than the happiest who will be born in our Peace-Union thousands of years after my departure. With this consolation every reader should follow my example and act with us for the introduction of the New Era.

After these hints some rules must be mentioned regarding the economy and management of affairs for the introduction and maintenance of the Peace-Union to realize what in Christ's peaceable reign on earth is expected.

As soon as circumstances will admit, a printing-office will be established on the place on which we commence our provisional Peace-Union centre, and a Periodical based on and directed by the principle of free discussion will be published, as the nature of the case, reason and arguments for the restoration of human rights demand. And previous steps, made before we are enabled to publish the Periodical, are subject to be criticized in the Periodical, and we undertake such enterprises or actions as we are ready to support before the tribunal of truth and righteousness.

This rule contains all that a sensible man or woman using his or her intellectual and moral faculties may demand. If we had used our whole book to develop our plan, we would not have finished our work, if the volume had been much larger than it is. But the points belonging to our plan, must be gradually developed in our Periodical, and those who comprehend this book and our mission, superabundance of credentials of which are contained here, will not tarry for a moment to co-operate with all their strength with us, and to draw their mortal and their departed friends into our Peace-Union.

Members of the Peace-Union agree to support whatever may be shown by free discussion through our Periodical to be suitable, practicable and necessary to promote the common welfare of the Peace-Union, which is the welfare of mankind. Those who would refuse to support it, had to show the contrary in the same Periodical, that it might be discussed, otherwise they would be disturbers, and if they could be by no means corrected, they would deserve to be excluded, and the Peace-Union, after having exhausted the means to bring them to the right order, would be compelled to declare them to be separated, and to give them the note or the certificate of their claim according to the rule above, and they return the receipt which they have obtained when they have brought their property into the Peace-Union.

We illustrate the point with an example. I have given, for instance, some hints regarding the two departments of males separately and females separately, notwithstanding the true matrimony of one husband with one wife. When there is the right time for them to procreate a child, they will have a convenient place for the performance of the most responsible duty. This my hint, when sufficiently explained, will satisfy every friend of progression into truth, righteousness and happiness, and will give to the human affairs quite a new turn, and deliver both sexes from temptations, in which until now the whole human race succumbed and descended much under the degree of the nobler classes of brutes, and parents depraved and ruined themselves and children. From all the strange and unexpected things disclosed in this book readers may expect that I have also regarding the true matrimony and the restitution of mankind in such a condition in which they will be truly happy, a glorious message and such truths which when sufficiently explained, will satisfy all lovers of progression into the true happiness. But there may join with our

Peace-Union some self-conceited person who would not give up what would be shown by us as necessary to be removed for the restoration of mankind to their true happiness, and what he would not be able to refute, and notwithstanding this he would remain in his bad habit. In this case he would compel us to remove him. At his removal he receives the note or certificate, while he returns the receipt which he had obtained for what he had put into the Peace-Union, as is explained above. But we have to add here, that if those who would be separated, had damaged the whole Peace-Union or some individual, the damage is to be deducted from their claim. And it is to be repeated, that nobody who joins with the Peace-Union, has any claim to any pay or reward for the labor performed in the Peace-Union, into which all men and women are invited to come and to remain in it in this mortal body and in all eternity, and to partake for him or her and their families of all riches, spiritual and physical in exchange for what they furnish. But what they brought in at their joining, is returned to them, with deduction of the damages, if they have caused any at their turn into enemies of the Peace-Union, or which originated by their fault, although it could not be proved, that they had a malicious intention in causing damages. This point is here to be remarked, that children before they acquire the legal age, if by whatever means they would be withdrawn from the Peace-Union, while their parents are living there or did not depart, should not receive the portion of the property brought for them into the Peace-Union, till they arrive at the legal age in which they have the right according to the laws of the country to depart from their parents; because the Peace-Union have the parental duties towards children who are received with their parents into the Peace-Union. Also this is to be mentioned, that no others except who come with their parents or with their children into the Peace-Union, have any claim to the property which they bring into it. They settle their business with all others, when they join with the Peace-Union, and in the same time they make their will, how much they themselves if they would leave the Peace-Union and some of their children would remain in it, and how much eaeh of the children when in full legal age, would receive, if he or she would leave the Peace-Union.

We thought proper to concede so much to the feebleness of those who are desirous to join with the Peace Union, but imagine the possible case, that they might be turned out and lose their property. For them their property is secured, althought without interest, and their possible case is rather imagination, and they would become gradually so strong as to give good example to others. But we have mentioned a point which must terrify hypocrites to join to our Peace Union; because their hypocrisy would become in due time manifest, and then they could not stand and would be turned out with demand to repair damages. Therefore they should remain in Babylon till they have a sincere desire to join with us for their true conversion to our principles and corresponding acting with us. When they are determined to act for this purpose they should not be afraid to join the Peace Union on account of the possibility of being separated; because no person will be separated except such as deserves in consequence of immoral acts or gross omissions of what is absolutely necessary for obtaining the object of our association, after having been sufficiently instructed and exhorted that their toleration would ruin the Peace Union. A separate person, if he or she would think there was not sufficient cause for separation, will be permitted to publish in our Periodical the reason or reasons of his or her complaint, By doing so, however, he gives occasion for members of the Peace Union to publish their remarks on his reasons, that truth might be made manifest; because the object of the Peace Union is the restoration of human rights, and therefore her members engage and promise to correct any mistake, when it is shown and it is proven.

The nature and object of the Peace Union is, that science or knowledge in every department and every branch of enterprise directs and governs the work. Therefore the man or woman who is found to be most skilful in any art, business or work, is to be elected as foreman, and continues to act as such, till some one more skilful is found. And then to him the place is to be given, however, not before it is shown, that by exchanging the place sufficient advantage will accrue to the community. The member who thinks he is able to show this, may assemble members belonging to the branch of that business, or if the case is a general case, members in general, the body of females having their votes as well as the body of males in general affairs; in particular branches the body decide who belong to that branch. Whoeveer calls members together, shows them the case, and if the majority find his reasons to be sufficient, the person proposed obtains the office. But before votes are taken, those who are assembled, must also hear the objections. But if there is any member who thinks, that the decision was not made according to justice, he may announce the matter to the assembled, showing them their mistake and his duty that if they will not correct their mistake, he will make known the reasons of his complaint against the decision in the Periodical of the Peace Union. And the assembled, if they see that he is right, are bound to receive thankfully that which is right, but if they see that he is wrong, they are bound to show him this. But if he, notwithstanding this, publishes his reasons, those who do not agree with him, are bound to show in their replies that he will not act according to sound reasons, but is disposed to make disturbance, deserving to be expelled. In this case if he continues to be obstinate against evidence, he should be expelled peaceably.

In the first place we need a centre. And according to the pattern of the centre as many settlements on other places will be established as will be needed to accommodate all who will find best to move from their present situation to a settlement of our Peace Union. But everywhere persons of our principles will be needed to instruct and strengthen the neighbours. The hints given here will be so modified to their situation as their circumstances will require.

In the centre is to be concentrated, what is to be spread everywhere, to benefit in the first place members of the Peace Union and by their instrumentality as many others as can be reached. Therefore co-operation and support from all who comprehend this book and their application to others is necessary to raise means, for establishing what is required in the centre. Although all who contribute for the centre, will not have chance to reside there, they will have a chance to send some of their children or relations to the institutions of the University for the New Era, which will be established there, according to our plan, according to which a great change will take place in studies, that all intellectual and moral faculties of students will be harmoniously developed, and much time will be gained for learning every day for some hours in the school and for some hours in the shops and elsewhere that to learn which each will be most qualified and inclined. Wherefore those who afford money and other property for the centre and what is needed there, acquire the right to reside there, when needed as teachers, or for mechanical branches, arts, sciences, for agriculture, horticulture, &c. What mankind need for the New Era, should be shown there to students theoretically and practically. Therefore all who have superabundant means, if they comprehend this book, will send such an amount as they can spare, as donations, which will become spiritual treasures to the donors. When the institutions which according to our plan should be at our centre, will be established, there will be such competition of students, that there will not be room for accommodation of all. All that is given as donation for raising our institutions, will be put in our ledger for the benefit of the donors, so that, when all students could not be accommodated at our centre, those recommended by the donors would be prefered to others, the case excepted, that others be found more useful in our mission, if they study the branches.

Those who have no superabundance of means to give a donation, are invited to invest for establishing the centre as much as their cicumstances permit, to be invested for their benefit, as belonging to them, although without any interest in money, but with the advantage, that when all students could not be accommodated at our centre, their sons and daughters would have the preference before such as have done nothing towards the foundation of the centre. And if any have land, who are desirous that on their land a settlement might be started according to our plan for the New Era, by their furnishing means for starting the centre they acquire the claim and right that their land shall be taken for that purpose rather than the land of another who had done nothing for the centre, when circumstances would not require the preference of the land of other for a new settlement of our Peace Union.

From what has been mentioned, the following general rule may be derived : Without having a centre of our communities we cannot accomplish our work. Therefore all who comprehend us, are solemnly entreated to contribute without delay what their circumstances allow. If they cannot send a donation, they are entreated to send what will be regarded as theirs without bearing interests, but bearing to them all the advantages to which according to the circumstances they are qualified, to come, when all will be prepared, to the centre, if they can be employed there; otherwise they may be useful to our community on the place which they now occupy, or they may join with an other place of our community. In this case the centre settles with that community in reference to what they have advanced to the centre, to be sent, when the centre is able to do so, to that community for them, if they should not prefer to leave it in the centre to be consumed there by such students as they would send to the University in the centre of our Peace Union, where all the knowledge and wisdom which can be obtained, will be concentrated to bring mankind into that situation which is promised and mankind are able to attain by the right application of their intellectual and moral faculties and their physical strength, and the proper use and right application of all the knowledge which has been propagated through the course of centuries and improved in our age.

No money or other property can or will be taken into the Peace Union settlements to be put into their ledger for the benefit of the person who invests it, to be returned in the case that the person or one of his or her family should leave the Peace-Union, except money that has been acquired in an honest manner. By the term *honest* we mean a manner which is not only justifiable according to the laws of the country, but also according to the moral laws attributable to the person who invests it, at least so far, that no person or society is known to whom it should be restored. We do not mean the severest scrutiny, but the usual course of affairs; because according to our plan by those who will join the Peace Union, the way will be opened for a final restoration of all human affairs into the right order. To this point we must gradually proceed.

By what we have remarked in regard to money as the root of all evil, if it is not managed for the commom welfere, it is a necessary evil as far as business is done with those who do not belong to our Peace Union, and we are compelled to make use of many evils which are yet in existence, to bring nations out of the evil into the New Era. We must make such use of money as to promote the welfere of the Peace Union which encloses the welfere of all nations, which would not be promoted, if we would take any amount of money from those who enter into our Peace Union under the condition to return it in case, they would leave the Peace Union. Under this condition we could take no more than one thousand dollars, so that, if any man or woman would come with his or her family, and bring more than one thousand dollars for each person belonging to his or her family, after having settled all matters of business with others, we could not take more than the mentioned sum under the mentioned condition, to wit, if husband and wife with parents and children, would join, for each of them one thousand dollars; the surplus they had to give as donation, if they would not accept the advice which is given below.

Also this is to be mentioned, that if a family comes on the place of the Peace Union and they invest for each member of the family a certain sum, and some of the family would be taken into the spirit world, and the others would leave the Peace Union, in this case only that has been invested for them, would belong to them. What was given for the departed, remains in the Peace Uuion. Also in the case, that a father would come with a large or with a small family and give for each individual a certain sum, and then the others would remain, but he himself would become a backslider, his claim would be only to the money which he had invested for his own person. The same priciple is to be applied in every case, in which somebody invests a certain sum for himself, and besides also sums for others.

To those who have greater riches than one thousand dollars for each individual of their family, is to be said, that they are only adminsitrators of that property to make the poor rich and the rich truly happy. And whereas the Peace-Union undertakes this great work, a rich person should be instructed and enlightened, that this will not take place in any other way than by a true community, for which we have given this sketch, only in this point deviating from the course which we would pursue if we would have to deal with perfect persons, that we found proper to concede, that if any body should leave the Peace-Union settlement, he should receive in due time the sum invested not exceeding one thousand dollars. But those whose property reaches higher, will go the safest way according to Christ's direction: "Go thy way, sell whatever thou hast and give to the poor, and thou shalt have treasure in Heaven; and come and take up thy cross and follow me." Mark x: 21. This man to whom Christ gave that advice" had great possessions." And we give to those who have great riches the same advice, but with a different application. Jesus Christ, the Father of the New Era which is to be introduced by our mission, had not the chance in Palestine, which we have in the United States. He advised as he could in his circumstances, and we give in our circumstances to the rich who have great possessions the following advice and the best for them to be saved: "Give as a donation as much into our Peace-Union centre as you are able to do for raising our institutions as the best means for the redemption of the poor and degraded people from the existing misery and distress, and come and learn how to administer your possessions for the poor, and we will send with you to your poseessions a man to commence there with you a community for the poor only, and you may call poor people of your choice together. And you should superintend, and our administrator should assist you and labor with you to educate the poor so as to make them truly rich and happy. And you, while you would have enriched our centre as much as would be possible without selling your possessions, would be the presiding elder at the community of the poor made rich by your possessions, and when you would be pleased to stop with those in the centre, you would be received as one of the founders, and you would "have treasure in Heaven,"

What I say to one I say to all rich men und women. If they receive our advice they will become very rich and happy; but now they are "wretched and miserable and poor and blind and naked," Revelation iii: 17. They are the Heads in Laodicea, which means the judgment of the people, whom they are preparing for destruction, and for themselves the hell. Luke xvi: 23. From them is more required to be saved than from those who have only a small property in comparison with the great possessions of the rich, and their small property they have earned with hard labor. But it would be too troublesome to reckon, how they had acquired their riches. But instead of a long reckoning or a general confession of their sins and crimes we show them the shortest and surest way to Heaven.

We must say also to those who invest property not exceeding one thousand dollars for each member of their family into our Peace-Union with the reserve that if they leave the Peace-Union, that property should be returned to them in equivalent without any interest, and at a time in which the Peace-Union can easily do this without hurting their own business, that this reserve will continue only until the time in which they will be sufficiently strengthened in the principles of the true community, and convinced that this is the only way for redemption of oppressed humanity. When they will advance so far, they will sign the covenant of the New Era, they themselves and those of their family who are of age and with them united in the Spirit; and they will transfer the property which is their portion to the community, which secures their rights to the provisions for their body and their spirit to enjoy such happiness as the Peace-Union will be able to afford to prepare them for the society of blessed spirits.

From these hints you see, that the true community consists of members who give all their property, without any reserve, and receive all the advantages which a mutual co-operation in the true brotherly spirit affords. At the commencement they must be tried. On the title-page of this book we have mentioned, that it is published at the "Peace-Union Centre." We intended to give explanation of the matter in this plan. We are starting there the Peace-Union Centre.

About five hundred acres of land, with farmhouse, barn, orchard &c. belong to that property, on a beautiful very healthy hill, with excellent springs of soft water, romantic locations for buildings, and all kinds of institutions for the New Era. The soil as far as may be cleared, is good for raising all kinds of fruits, and as much as we will need of vegetables. But our centre will be for literary institutions, surrounded with all kinds of the best mechanics and artists, from whom students will learn all kinds of work. Therefore the largest portion of grain will be obtained from other settlements to which productions at the centre will be sent in exchange. About one hundred acres of the land are cleared and much more can be cleared and used for different purposes, but the largest portion of that land is Toscarora mountain, producing wood, timber, stone for building, and is good for different other purposes, for instance, the top of the mountain for our observatory, &c.

Spring Hill in Racoon Valley belonged to Abraham, the oldest of the twelve sons of my departed friend Christian Long. Christian was one of the students of my German books, and strong witness of our mission; but his son Abraham preaching water baptism was not prepared to receive his testimony. But Christian and others in his company amongst the departed, were operating and preparing this place, while we thought that we had already succeeded in taking another place in possession, seventeen miles from this place, and we have been in quite an unexpected manner instructed that Springhill is the place in which we should start the Peace-Union Centre, and we have received the place as cheap as the worth of its improvements may be valued This is according to our principles, according to which the land belongs to the whole human family, and to the improvements only each individual may claim as much right as he has consumed labor to produce them. But it is evident also that labor never can be exactly valued, and I had to write a very large volume to expose the manifold forms of labor, in which time is wasted, to corrupt and ruin human society. All the hints given in this book, may convince any investigating mind, that there is no redemption of the degraded and wretched condition of mankind except in the community in which men will be brought gradually into the true happy state in this life and in the spirit world, and will draw their departed friends into higher spheres.

Being compelled by circumstances to take away manuscript containing the spirit battle by which not only this, that we have to start our Peace-Union as a community and in Springhill, but also many other important points have been disclosed, which although they were known to us long time before that, may arouse the attention of those who would not hear us otherwise, except when they hear extraordinary spirit manifestations, which in connexion with starting our Peace-Union Centre on this place may be published another time. But here we must mention that by quite an unexpected vision against the wishes of the medium and his wife our doctrine has been illustrated, to wit, that those who make a covenant with our Peace-Union community, separate so from those who remain in Babylon, that if of those who are married, one partner would make such a covenant, but the other would remain in Babylon, we would do all in our power to draw also that partner into our community. But if he or she would remain obstinate despiser of our Heavenly message, we according to Divine law would consider the person who made the covenant with our Peace-Union as perfectly free to marry a person belonging to our community, and labor at the same time to convert the Government to acknowledge our mission and the Divine law made manifest by our mediumship. "What God hath joined together let no man put asunder." Matth. xix: 6. "What the devil has joined together, God puts asunder." If we have the mission expressed on the title-page, and confirmed by all signs and wonders which have been mentioned in this book, and with which hundreds of volumes could be filled, then it is evident that the devil has joined those together or the devil will keep them together, when one understands our mission and advances so far that he or she makes the covenant with our community and the other resists and will keep him or her in Babylon, when he or she starts to come out of her not to be partaker of her sins. The partner, may be he or she, who remains obstinate, remains in the great whore of the 17th chapter of the Revelation, is an adulterer or adulteress in the spiritual sense, and certainly with whoredom or other abominations he or she became so endarkened, that when the partner progressed so far, as to comprehend our Heavenly message, the destroying devil will detain him or her from the truth made manifest in our message. Those who have comprehended this book to this point, know that our case is just the contrary to the so called Free Love, diametrically opposed to it. A chaste husband or wife will comprehend us, but those who will continue in their fornication and adultery, will cry against us and misrepresent truth for their destruction. Here is no room for explanation of a point, on which I will write an extraordinary treatise, in which I will report and explain also the mentioned vision, when the diseased stomachs will be ready to digest our most wholesome medicine.

In this compression is also to be remembered, that the promise given on the 45th page in regard to the four in Baltimore executed in connexion with my visit to President Buchanan appears in a more dreadful shape in the portion of the 4th treatise which will appear in the second edition of this book if that edition shall be demanded, than I would have expected, when I mentioned that case. When President Buchanan, Governor Hicks and other Grandees of Washington and Maryland were not prepared to afford money for buying Springhill for our Peace Union Centre and for publishing this book, we read on the 42d page: "The same time a great sign was given so that I was sent speedily from Baltimore to the Western Reserve of Ohio." A. D. 1854 we commenced to prepare Brother Robert D. Eldrige in Baltimore for our mission. Then happened many wonders and signs in connexion with him, till at length a sign was given in Baltimore. But the principal of the four executed in Baltimore was brought before me in the Western Reserve of Ohio, and you will hear of strange spectacles in the next edition regarding that manifestation in connexion with the four Presidents Taylor, Fillmore, Pierce and Buchanan. After having performed the trials of spirits in the Western Reserve of Ohio, Eldrige started with me, and after having tried spirits in different places during our travelling, we arrived at length at Abraham Long's, and I showed to Brother Eldrige some of the secret treasures on the premises of Springhill, where Heavenly Wisdon prepared a great variety of most beautiful sceneries, magnificent fairviews on a number of sites very suitable for excellent buildings, and to all those places excellent springs of soft water may be derived by few rods of pipes, and excellent stone for buildings and superabundance of wood is most handy. We took then the deeds in the name of our Peace Union Commnuity, and we appear as Trustees, I by virtue of my mission, in duty bound to communicate the spirit who has sent me for the fulfilment of the most glorious promises to mankind, with those who will receive this spirit and will be drawn from Babylon into the New Jerusalem, and Robert D. Eldrige by virtue of his mission, who came with money and paid for the place with the rights which are given in this plan to those who invest money, and with the duty of superintendency for a good success. In those our duties all are bound to support us, who join with the Peace Union.

On the 11th day of July, 1859, my Document, entitled : "Great News for the Friends of Progression in Truth and Righteousness towards the promised New Era of Harmony and Peace amongst all nations" was set in type, the proof-sheet corrected by me, and a portion of copies struck off on the same day. We were preparing readers for the first convention which will be held in the New Hall on the Peace Union settlement in the latter part of the next month, and requesting Editors to publish that Document. But I think that the warlike spirit of destruction kept most of them in the servitude of monarchs. But that document was to be set in type and printed on the same day, on which Napoleon and Francis Joseph made their treaty of peace at Villafranca for an important testimony, that spirits from our sphere have controlled the affairs also there, so that if you hurry to do what is required in this book, you will prevent immense destruction of human life and property in this country, otherwise you should know that I have done more than from a mortal man could be expected, to move you for action. But when men become such beasts that they have no sense for spiritual things, destruction is a necessary consequence. At the commencement of the first treatise page 6 you see that Mr. Belly gave occasion to that treatise. Last month he came again to Paris and remains there according to newspapers until the 20th of the next month; and I proposed that on the same day our first convention should commence in the New Hall. We quote from said document in which the title of this book is copied, the close as follows: "The book with the above copied title will be published by Robert D. Eldrige in our Convention, and then copies will be sent by him to those who send to him the money (50 cents for one copy, twenty dollars for 50 copies, 35 dollars for 100 copies) either before or after or at the Convention. He being a man of property and known as our trusty fellow labourer for improving the condition of mankind, has charge of the business department at our Peace Union, while, I the writer of this book and of this article am bound to devote my precious time to spiritual objects for Harmony and Peace of Nations, requesting to direct letters which do not belong particularly to my sphere, to him under the direction: Robert D. Eldrige, Donnally's Mill, Perry Co: Pa." This book appears small for this price; but remember the contents of page 169, and collect subscribers, and as soon as we print the second edition, we will send a large pamphlet as supplement without additional charge. In the mean time we assure you that also this small book contains so large an amount of most important points for you, that the oftener you study it, the more you will learn to appreciate its value; and the enormous labour for obtaining all the parts contained in this book cannot be paid with money, and my labour never was paid.

On the 11th of this month, August, 1859, there came many people to Springhill An extraordinary medium who had been in England an Elder amongst the Baptisers wrote on the 13th Instant to me: "I came on foot to Springhill, Peace Union Centre, a long walk of about 17 miles in hot weather. We raised the frame work of the Large Hall. The day (11th inst.) was fine, and all things went on well, and the work that is done, looks well and in good order. All kinds of rumors and talk: What the house is for?

What they will do? Why did they not build so as the Hall could be seen? Some one thing, some, other things, &c."

The Periodical, entitled: "Peace Union Message." Conventions at the Peace Union Centre in Springhill, Toscarora Township, Perry Co: Pa. 6 miles west of Millerstown, the stopping place for the Cars.

Our Periodical, spoken of in the plan, will be published as soon, as there will be a sufficient number of subscribers. In the expectation that those who are versed in English, will comprehend us first, we will publish it first in English, in Quarto, to be preserved in books and translated in as many other languages as needed; because it will contain social, ecclesiastical and political matters and movements of nations and daily news of importance, considered from our position, to draw nations from the existing confusion and degradation into the new order of things. All that will improve the condition of mankind, and what is hurtful for them, as far as we will have oportunity to reach it, will be examined from our position. But there not being room in this book, we will publish in the first number which will issue, when we are secured by subscriptions, what we will find proper to draw those amongst all nations who have somewhat new for improving mankind, to send it for publication in our Periodical. Every one who sends somewhat of this kind, will add his full direction and occupation. If his or her communication is found by those whom we find to be competent judges in that branch, to be such as required, it will be published when room will be for it in our Periodical. But if it is not found such as to be published, the writer will be named and the reason given, why it cannot be published. If the writer should think to have been injured, our Periodical would be open to publish his complaint with the preliminary requisites which will be made known in our first number as quite reasonable to save time to him and us and to the readers as well as to the printers and others. I quoted purposely some passages from the letter of our friend Peter assuring that he is ours truly "in bonds for truth waiting for deliverance." If the talkers of nonsense had asked those to whom we told, why we selected that place for that building, near the farm house and the springs, they had received information. The basement of the new building is a large cellar, the first story a large Hall, having in the midst a partition, which we remove when we use the whole Hall, but the second story has a partition which cannot be removed and each department has its own stairs. The farm house and the new building are in a cove The first story of the building will be provisionaly used for our Conventions, till the substantial edifice within the most magnificent fairview will be established. With this fairview we entreat most earnestly every reader to collect as many subscribers for this book as well as for the Periodical, as he or she is able to collect. The book is to be paid for at the delivery, and the Periodical will cost $2 a year, money to be paid for half a year or a year at the delivery of the first number.

Whoever secures us five subscribers receives six copies. And those who will act as agents, after having comprehended by studying this book our plan and adopt it, are regarded as our fellow-laborers, when they show practically that they belong to our Peace-Union. If the expected exertions are made, we may be able to publish the first number of our Periodical at the commencement of the year 1860.

Our first Convention next month at the Peace Union Centre is announced in our Circular. But readers of this book are requested to proclaim, that on the first day of November 1859, the second Convention will commence and continue for two weeks, and that only those persons of both sexes are invited to attend, who after having comprehended our mission are ready to act as missionaries or to support with their means our enterprises to establish what is needed at the Centre. And for this purpose we intend to hold successively a number of Conventions. The second could be attended by those who belong to the Cabinet and the Congress of Washington, or to any legislature. Each Convention will last one or two weeks. Those who comprehend this book will tell or write to those with whom they are acquainted, that although the contents of this book are of importance for any body, those who belong to the Government need most to understand them. This book will be taken as the text-book, but also those who may have read it before many times, will receive in the Convention new light to understand it better and to hear many things which are not mentioned in the book. There may be so many aroused to attend the Convention that all could not be accommodated. Therefore whoever and whenever he determines to attend one of our Conventions, he is requested to write directly, and to give an exact direction, and put a letter stamp into his letter, and we will answer it, and tell, whether he could be accommodated in that or in any of the following Conventions Boarding is to be had as moderately as we can afford it. The rule is to be observed also afterwards in this and in the next year, that whoever wishes to attend our Convention, is requested to write directly, and he will receive an answer when he could be accommodated. Answer may come sooner or later, because it may depend upon circumstances, when after the receipt of his or her letter our next Convention would be held. Probably there is in this last " form " no room, to say more than that our Post-Office address is on the title-page and also three or four pages before this. It has been said that the stopping place for the cars is Millerstown, Perry Co. : Pa. I desire nothing more than to draw you into the sphere of our Heavenly abode as your sincere brother.

ANDREW B. SMOLNIKAR.

Remark. I perused 192 pages of this book while the last form was in composition, and found a moderate number of errata as may be easily corrected by the reader; for instance, he may connect himself in the 7th line of the "Preliminary Remarks" the two particles IN TO in one word, and he may separate where he finds two words close together and change C and E, also N and U and some other letters when required, or add when a letter is omitted, or cast it out when it is superabundant Such trifles will not trouble those who are anxious to learn to understand this book, nor if they read sometimes CONNEXION and other times CONNECTION. I always write CONNEXION; but I was assured, that according to the present fashion CONNECTION is more used, although this use is irregular.

The general rule is observed by our invisible messengers mentioned on the 169th page, while they are controlling the spirits of the compositors, that they let them commit such errata as disturb the sense on such pages, on which the reader should stop and reflect upon the connexion of matters. An astonishing lesson was given, when I received the order to stop the composition of the Fourth Treatise at the end of the 168th page. The manuscript for that Treatise contains 85 pages, and the 168th page of this book ends in the middle of the 34th page of manuscript. The spirit who made this provision exhorts powerfully readers to digest the 168 pages and to prepare for what follows. I did not know, what our invisible agents intended to put on the 168th page, till I saw in the proof sheet the six oxen, the first of whom is Joseph Ox, on the 74th place of our catalogue. These oxen are supporting the mysteries on the 80th and 81st places of our catalogue, and those two mysteries are in the 4th line of the 168th page. This provision tells that you should pay peculiar attention to the contents from the 74th to the 81st page of this book, and you will find amongst the Americans those who furnish as great assistance to the Beast with ten horns as the six oxen on the 168th page. But on the 21st line of the 82d page, my interpretation commences, and the omission in the midst of the 83d page exhorts you that you should reflect upon the "Sect of Adventurists" mentioned in the 9th line from the bottom of the 83d page. In my manuscript were only Adventists. But I tell you that the young boy who set in type the largest portion of this book, was a peculiar medium. Noyse and Himes and all those whom they represent belong to the sect of Adventurists who are the greatest supporters of Popery.

All other marvellous things you will hear in our Convention commencing November 1, 1859, on the Feast of All Saints.

My address is page 124 of this book.

Set in type June 27th, 1859.

www.ingramcontent.com/pod-product-compliance
Lightning Source LLC
LaVergne TN
LVHW011214110826
845150LV00006B/1433

* 9 7 8 1 4 2 5 5 1 6 7 6 5 *